Molinist Philosophical and Theological Ventures

Molinist Philosophical and Theological Ventures

Kirk R. MacGregor

☙PICKWICK *Publications* · Eugene, Oregon

MOLINIST PHILOSOPHICAL AND THEOLOGICAL VENTURES

Copyright © 2022 Kirk R. MacGregor. All rights reserved. Except for brief quotations in critical publications or reviews, no part of this book may be reproduced in any manner without prior written permission from the publisher. Write: Permissions, Wipf and Stock Publishers, 199 W. 8th Ave., Suite 3, Eugene, OR 97401.

Pickwick Publications
An Imprint of Wipf and Stock Publishers
199 W. 8th Ave., Suite 3
Eugene, OR 97401

www.wipfandstock.com

PAPERBACK ISBN: 978-1-6667-3030-2
HARDCOVER ISBN: 978-1-6667-2160-7
EBOOK ISBN: 978-1-6667-2161-4

Cataloguing-in-Publication data:

Names: MacGregor, Kirk R. [author]

Title: Molinist philosophical and theological ventures / Kirk R. MacGregor.

Description: Eugene, OR: Pickwick Publications, 2022 | Includes bibliographical references and index.

Identifiers: ISBN 978-1-6667-3030-2 (paperback) | ISBN 978-1-6667-2160-7 (hardcover) | ISBN 978-1-6667-2161-4 (ebook)

Subjects: LCSH: Molinism | Free will and determinism—Religious aspects—Christianity | Religion—Philosophy | Philosophy | God (Christianity)—Omniscience

Classification: BT762 M33 2022 (print) | BT762 (ebook)

09/28/22

Unless otherwise noted, Scripture quotations are from New Revised Standard Version Bible, copyright © 1989 National Council of the Churches of Christ in the United States of America. Used by permission. All rights reserved worldwide.

Scripture quotations marked NIV are taken from the Holy Bible, New International Version®, NIV®. Copyright © 1973, 1978, 1984, 2011 by Biblica, Inc.® Used by permission of Zondervan. All rights reserved worldwide. www.zondervan.com The "NIV" and "New International Version" are trademarks registered in the United States Patent and Trademark Office by Biblica, Inc.®

To Dee Erway-Sherwood, Professor of Art and Executive Director of Visual and Digital Arts at McPherson College

Contents

List of Illustrations | ix
Acknowledgments | xi
Introduction | xiii

1. Molinism and the Bible: Part One | 1
2. Molinism and the Bible: Part Two | 21
3. An Intuitionist Defense of Divine Supercomprehension | 38
4. Critiquing Explanatory Priority Arguments against Molinism | 57
5. A Molinist Interpretation of Alleged Open Theist Prooftexts | 76
6. The Logical Consistency of Molinism on Branching Time Models | 91
7. Molinism, Apologetics, and Music | 107
8. The Relationship between Molinism and Eventual Universalism | 117

Conclusion | 135
Bibliography | 139
Subject Index | 147
Scripture Index | 155

List of Illustrations

Figure 1 | 65

Figure 2 | 67

Figure 3 | 92

Figure 4 | 96

Figure 5 | 98

Figure 6 | 99

Figure 7 | 101

Figure 8 | 102

Figure 9 | 102

Figure 10 | 103

Figure 11 | 104

Figure 12 | 104

Acknowledgments

I WOULD LIKE TO thank all my colleagues at McPherson College for creating an ideal atmosphere of warmth and friendship that cultivates my ability to teach in the classroom and through my publications. I owe a special debt of gratitude to President Michael Schneider and Provost and Executive Vice President Amanda Gutierrez for their unflinching support of my research. Thanks to Tom Hurst, my colleague in the Department of Philosophy and Religion, for his constant encouragement. I am especially grateful to Dee Erway-Sherwood, Professor of Art and Executive Director of Visual and Digital Arts, for her tremendous assistance with producing the graphics in chapters four and six. She taught me the basics of Adobe Illustrator and helped me in the computer lab whenever I had technical difficulties, which was extremely often. This book is rightfully dedicated to her.

Most importantly, I would like to thank my wife Lara and my son Dwiane. In addition to her unfailing love, Lara regularly discusses philosophical and theological matters with me and gives me valuable insights. Dwiane's constant love, joy, and energy motivates me in my writing.

Introduction

THIS BOOK IS A collection of essays on Molinist philosophical and theological topics whose aim is to demonstrate the biblical foundations of Molinism, rebut various contemporary challenges to Molinism, and expand the scope of Molinism to new areas of interest. Here I will furnish a brief outline of the book's contents.

Chapters one and two firmly establish Molinism's scriptural credentials. As prerequisite to this task, I address the proper relationship between theology and philosophy. Laying out the biblical data on five loci—divine sovereignty, human freedom, predestination, grace, and God's salvific will—I insist, in line with biblical inerrancy, that no locus of Scripture be subordinated to any other locus or that its original meaning (i.e., the meaning intended by the pertinent biblical author or authors) be explained away in order to accommodate some other locus. As part of loving God with all our minds, I use philosophy as theology's handmaiden to integrate loci that, while not contradicting each other, do not themselves explain how they relate to one another. I show how the tenets of Molinism naturally and gradually unfold in the process. In so doing, I make the case that the best and most faithful explanation of the biblical data is Molinism.

After surveying and briefly analyzing various proffered—and in my judgment successful—responses to the grounding objection, chapter three proceeds, with the unwitting help of Francisco Suárez, to develop a new response. Accordingly, counterfactuals of creaturely freedom (CCFs) are

Introduction

grounded in God's justified and warranted beliefs about what the actualization of libertarian creaturely essences would do in every conceivable circumstance. These beliefs arise from God's intuition, understood as a cognitive faculty for making cogent judgments in evidentially underdeterminative cases. Enlisting the help of scholars from various disciplines, I construct this conception of intuition and show its applicability in the case of finite human minds and, by analogy, in the case of the infinite divine mind whose image the human mind represents. Identifying God's intuition as the means for his supercomprehension, I then respond to various objections to the doctrine, including its supposed prevention of God from possessing complete self-knowledge and its allegedly leading to determinism.

Chapter four delineates and refutes recent objections to Molinism based on the notion of explanatory priority and levied by Philip Swenson, Nevin Climenhaga, and Daniel Rubio. Regarding Swenson, I first argue that the principle of the Fixity of the Independent on which his objections are based at crucial points is, from a Molinist perspective, either incoherent, false, or trivially true. As such, it holds no purchase against Molinism. I proceed to show that neither horn of Swenson's dilemma against Molinism, according to which Molinism is respectively deterministic or viciously circular, succeeds. I then disclose that Swenson's argument against Molinism based on the unchangeability of divine intentions misses the mark due to its failure to appreciate the distinction between changing the fact of God's intention, which cannot be done, and frustrating God's intention, which can be, and often is, done by free creatures. Regarding Climenhaga and Rubio, I contest their allegation that human actions are fully explained, and therefore determined, by the union of either CCFs and Creation or contingent facts about creaturely essences (which explain CCFs) and Creation. This allegation overlooks the very essence of agent causation. As such, their argument that Molinism issues forth in determinism fares no better than Swenson's.

The Molinist exegesis of divine relational changeability texts, or assertions that God faces situations different than or contrary to what he had anticipated, tests creatures to discover the level of their allegiance to him, "changes his mind," or "repents of" or "regrets" choices that he himself made, is the subject of chapter five. Observing that previous attempts to depict these texts as anthropomorphisms cannot disclose any literal truths to which they point, open theists standardly take these as prooftexts for their position. But can Molinism disclose such literal truths, so throwing new light on these passages? I contend that the answer is yes. In so doing, I

Introduction

challenge the Stalnaker-Lewis semantics for counterfactuals by arguing that so-called might counterfactuals and would-probably counterfactuals are actually statements of intrinsic probability. These are necessary truths and so known by God in his natural knowledge. The literal neological progression from what God knows in his natural knowledge to what God knows in his middle knowledge is metaphorically illustrated in texts that depict God as confronting unexpected situations, testing people, and changing his mind. Texts depicting God as regretting decisions can be understood in the same fashion or, alternatively, as literal statements of emotions God middle-knew he would feel upon actualizing the world but which were overridden by other emotions God also middle-knew he would feel.

Chapter six takes up Alex Malpass's challenge that Molinism is proven logically inconsistent by branching time models in three respects. These respects run as follows. First, in view of three consecutive temporal moments, there can be no truth value at the third moment to propositions expressing what, had a different future resulted from an event at the first moment, would have eventuated from a nonactual indeterminate event at the second moment. Second, Molinism causes the failure of tautologies about possible worlds containing compound tenses. Third, branching time models force Molinism to posit the absurdity of two different species of actuality. I argue that none of these objections is true. The first objection, I contend, is based on the false metaphysical assumption that time makes things happen rather than recording what things happen or being produced by things happening. The second objection, I contend, confuses the actual past (and future) with nonactual pasts (and futures). When these are differentiated, propositions about possible worlds containing compound tenses succeed on Molinism. The third objection, I contend, simply forces the Molinist to distinguish possibility, feasibility, and actuality, such that only the feasible world chosen by God is actual. In tackling this objection, I show how Molinism affords an illuminating account of branching time models, understood non-literally as heuristic devices, as illustrating the relationship between possible galaxies, possible futures, feasible futures, and feasible worlds.

Chapter seven brings Molinism into the uncharted waters of theological aesthetics. Bringing Molina into conversation with Karl Barth and Alvin Plantinga, I contend that music is not intrinsically holy but becomes holy when God chooses to imbue it with God's presence in order to effectuate a personal encounter with at least one other individual. God decides when to do this on the basis of God's middle knowledge. In cases where God

Introduction

middle-knows that if God were to imbue music with the divine presence, then the *sensus divinitatis* of at least one performer or hearer would function properly and at least one of these same performers or hearers would freely respond to the output of the *sensus divinitatis* by entering into relationship with God, God suffuses music with God's presence and makes it holy. Holy music affords persons who positively respond to it with knowledge—and not mere true belief—that God exists and that they have encountered God. As a result, music plays a powerful apologetic function.

Chapter eight explores the relationship between Molinism and the controversial thesis of eventual universalism, by which I mean the view that hell exists and that the lost go to hell but eventually learn from the error of their ways and turn to God, whereupon God ultimately gives them eternal life. Molina himself subscribed to what I dub the eternalist view, namely, that those who die in a lost state remain in hell forever, owing not to his philosophical theology but to his interpretation of Scripture. Most contemporary Molinist philosophers use Molinism to defend the eternalist view. On the other hand, R. Zachary Manis has recently argued that Molinism strongly implies eventual universalism, and Eric Reitan maintains that the doctrine of libertarian freedom (a Molinist *sine qua non*) guarantees the truth of eventual universalism. I attempt to bring clarity to this issue by defending three contentions. First, Molinism renders eternalism logically possible and not necessarily improbable. Second, Molinism renders eventual universalism logically possible and not necessarily improbable. Third, if humans possess libertarian freedom, then Molinism constitutes a prerequisite for the success of universalism. Accordingly, given Molinism, neither eternalism nor eventual universalism is ruled out. Further, any form of universalism that embraces libertarian human freedom requires Molinism. If Molinism is true, then the debate over the truth of eternalism versus the truth of eventual universalism can only be settled on biblical grounds, not philosophical ones.

In short, this book advances the philosophical and theological conversation surrounding Molinism on a number of fronts. In the process, it evidences Molinism's biblical fidelity, coherence, and applicability to areas outside the immediate confines of divine providence and predestination.

— 1 —

Molinism and the Bible

Part One

A FREQUENT CRITICISM OF Molinism alleges that Molinism is a human-made philosophical construct that does not logically follow from but is rather superimposed on the Bible in order to preserve libertarian human freedom at all costs. In the opening two chapters I aim to refute this criticism. To do so, I first address the proper relationship between philosophy and theology. This entails responding to the following questions: Are all philosophical constructs merely human-made, or are at least some of these human discoveries of truths ontologically grounded in the mind of God? If the latter, how can we tell the difference between the two? Can we appropriately use philosophy in biblical interpretation? Granting that philosophical constructs cannot legitimately be superimposed on Scripture, may we avail ourselves of them when they seem pertinent to the biblical text? With such questions answered, I then survey and analyze the biblical data on divine sovereignty, human freedom, predestination, grace, and God's salvific will. I will insist that, for each doctrinal locus, the affirmations of Scripture must be taken at face value, without subordinating any locus to another or explaining away any locus in terms of another. I believe that a sound model of biblical authority demands as much. Pointing out that none of the biblical affirmations logically stand in contradiction to the others, I will propose that loving God with all our minds impels us to use abductive reasoning—or inference to the best explanation—to synthesize these affirmations. I will contend that the Molinist structure is the logical outcome of such reasoning.

The Proper Relationship between Philosophy and Theology

Theology is, as Aquinas pointed out, the queen of the sciences.[1] It is the most advanced discipline of study, since it is the study of God, the greatest conceivable being. One should therefore expect theology, pursued correctly, to be quite complex. But often people want a theology that is simple. As Muslim friends and Jehovah's Witnesses have said to me, one appeal of their unitarian theology is how simple it is: God is one being and one person. Even a child, they remark, can understand that. It never ceases to amaze me how Muslims and Jehovah's Witnesses think such simplicity is a good thing or a sign that their theology is true. Rather, I view this as an obvious red flag that their theology is false. Let me illustrate by way of example. Suppose my fourth-grade son were to tell me that arithmetic is the highest level of mathematics, for even he can do arithmetic. I would reply that arithmetic is an extremely basic level of mathematics that needs to be mastered before he could do more advanced levels like geometry, algebra, and trigonometry, all of which need to be mastered before he could do the more advanced level of calculus, and so forth. In the same way, a theology that even a child can understand will inevitably fail to grasp the reality of who the Ultimate Being is.

In keeping with the calculus analogy, doing theology well presupposes that the doer has mastered several lesser sciences which constitute prerequisites to the theological endeavor. Aquinas argued, correctly in my judgment, that the greatest of these prerequisite sciences is philosophy. Philosophy, etymologically speaking, is the love (*philo-*) of wisdom (*sophia*). Loving something entails pursuing it. We may therefore define philosophy as the love and pursuit of wisdom. The scriptural data on wisdom is legion. The Bible distinguishes between two types of wisdom: wisdom as such, otherwise called "wisdom from above" (Jas 3:17); and counterfeit wisdom, otherwise called "the wisdom of the world" (1 Cor 1:20), "human wisdom" (1 Cor 2:13), and "earthly wisdom" (2 Cor 1:12). Scripture makes abundantly clear that wisdom as such is ontologically grounded in God and thus comes to us from God. As Daniel exclaimed: "Blessed be the name of God from age to age, for wisdom and power are his. He changes times and seasons, deposes kings and sets up kings; he gives wisdom to the wise and knowledge to those who have understanding" (Dan 2:20–21). Job conveys the same sentiment: "With God are wisdom and strength; he has counsel

---

1. Aquinas, *Summa Theologiae* 1.1.5.

and understanding" (Job 12:13). God claims that he "has put wisdom in the inward parts" and "given understanding to the mind" (Job 38:36; see 1 Kgs 3:28; 4:29; 5:12; 10:24; 2 Chr 9:3; 9:23; Ezra 7:25; Job 12:13; Eph 1:8–9, 17; Jas 1:5). Wisdom's rootedness in God is given its classical poetic expression in the eighth chapter of the book of Proverbs. There wisdom proclaims:

> The LORD created me at the beginning of his work, the first of his acts of long ago. Ages ago I was set up, at the first, before the beginning of the earth. When there were no depths I was brought forth, when there were no springs abounding with water. Before the mountains had been shaped, before the hills, I was brought forth—when he had not yet made earth and fields, or the world's first bits of soil. When he established the heavens, I was there, when he drew a circle on the face of the deep, when he made firm the skies above, when he established the foundations of the deep, when he assigned to the sea its limit, so that the waters might not transgress his command, when he marked out the foundations of the earth, then I was beside him, like a master worker; and I was daily his delight, rejoicing before him always, rejoicing in his inhabited world and delighting in the human race. (Prov 8:22–31)

Since it is clear that God never lacked wisdom, the poetic exclamation that God created wisdom "at the beginning of his work" and as "the first of his acts of long ago" literally means that wisdom is eternally existent in God and perhaps eternally generated by the mind of God. God is therefore "excellent in wisdom" (Isa 28:29), and the Spirit of the Lord is "the spirit of wisdom and understanding" (Isa 11:2). In his explication of spiritual gifts, Paul declared: "To one is given through the Spirit the utterance of wisdom, and to another the utterance of knowledge according to the same Spirit" (1 Cor 12:8). By his wisdom God created the universe, including the earth and all its creatures (Ps 104:24; Prov 3:19; Jer 10:12; 51:15). The New Testament explicitly identifies Jesus Christ as the "wisdom of God" (1 Cor 1:24, 30), "in whom are hidden all the treasures of wisdom and knowledge" (Col 2:4). The Gospel of John famously equates the preincarnate Christ with the Logos, the divine wisdom and supreme rational principle ordering the universe, through whom "all things came into being" (John 1:1–2, 10, 14; see Col 1:16). As displayed by his teachings and actions, Jesus is the embodiment of wisdom as such (Matt 11:19; 23:34; Mark 6:2; Luke 2:40; 7:35; 11:49).

Molinist Philosophical and Theological Ventures

Scripture exhorts human beings to acquire wisdom as such and warns of the danger of neglecting wisdom (Prov 1:20–33; 3:21; 4:10–11; 5:1; 7:4; 8:1–21; 9:13–18). Wisdom is a prerequisite to fearing and knowing God:

> My child, if you accept my words and treasure up my commandments within you, making your ear attentive to wisdom and inclining your heart to understanding; if you indeed cry out for insight, and raise your voice for understanding; if you seek it like silver, and search for it as for hidden treasures—then you will understand the fear of the Lord and find the knowledge of God. For the Lord gives wisdom; from his mouth come knowledge and understanding. (Prov 2:1–6)

Accordingly, the Bible commands us to engage in the task of philosophy, namely, the love and pursuit of wisdom: "Get wisdom; get insight; do not forget; nor turn away from the words of my mouth. Do not forsake her, and she will keep you; *love her*, and she will guard you. The beginning of wisdom is this: Get wisdom, and whatever else you get, get insight. Prize her highly, and she will embrace you; she will honor you if you embrace her" (Prov 4:5–8, emphasis added; see Prov 7:4). Likewise, wisdom personified states, "I love those who love me, and those who seek me diligently find me" (Prov 8:17). Wisdom pleads: "You that are simple, turn in here! . . . Come, eat of my bread and drink of the wine I have mixed. Lay aside immaturity, and live, and walk in the way of insight" (Prov 9:4–6). Solomon remarked: "How much better to get wisdom than gold! To get understanding is to be chosen rather than silver. . . . Wisdom is a fountain of life to one who has it, but folly is the punishment of fools" (Prov 16:16, 22; see Prov 23:33).

It follows from the foregoing discussion that the constructs of wisdom as such, and hence the constructs of philosophy done properly, are ontologically grounded in the divine mind rather than made by humans. To the degree that humans know these constructs, humans have discovered what is eternally present in God. Moreover, since wisdom is a prerequisite to knowing God, philosophy done properly is a prerequisite to doing theology. Hence Paul described his own theological agenda as follows: "It is he [Christ] whom we proclaim, warning everyone and teaching everyone in all wisdom, so that we may present everyone mature in Christ" (Col 1:28; see Col 3:16). Theology carried out with the assistance of philosophy is thus necessary for Christian maturity. As Paul stated elsewhere: "Yet among the mature we do speak wisdom, though it is not a wisdom of this age or of the rulers of this age, who are doomed to perish. But we speak God's wisdom, secret and hidden, which God decreed before the ages for our glory" (1 Cor 2:6–7). Indeed it is the responsibility of the church to "[make] known . . . the wisdom of God in its rich variety . . . to the rulers and authorities in the heavenly places" (Eph 3:10). Certainly the Bible knows nothing of a "philosophy-free" theology, as studying God apart from a necessary condition to knowing God—the love and pursuit of wisdom—is a contradiction in terms.[2]

At the same time, the Bible warns us against the love and pursuit of counterfeit wisdom, which Paul described as the "wisdom of this age" and of "the rulers of this age" (1 Cor 2:6). James epitomized this wisdom as envious and selfish in nature: "But if you have bitter envy and selfish ambition in your hearts, do not be boastful and false to the truth. Such wisdom does not come down from above, but is earthly, unspiritual, devilish. For where there is envy and selfish ambition, there will also be disorder and wickedness of every kind" (Jas 3:14–16). Paul rightfully denounced the love and pursuit of counterfeit wisdom as "hollow and deceptive philosophy, which depends on human tradition and the elemental spiritual forces of this world rather than on Christ" and admonished that we not be taken captive by it (Col 2:8 NIV).[3] Paul stressed the superiority of the wisdom of God, exemplified in Jesus' crucifixion, to the wisdom of the world in these words:

> Where is the one who is wise? Where is the scribe? Where is the debater of this age? Has not God made foolish the wisdom of the world? For since, in the wisdom of God, the world did not know God through wisdom, God decided, through the foolishness of

---

2. As the theologian Hans Boersma correctly emphasizes, "When we try to read Scripture apart from any metaphysical presuppositions whatsoever, our very attempt to exalt the Bible collapses in on itself. Faith isn't meant to function without reason, and we shouldn't attempt to do theology without philosophy. The isolation of Scripture vis-à-vis metaphysics is practically impossible: invariably it means the unwitting adoption of one metaphysic or another. . . . When we try to isolate Scripture from metaphysical presuppositions, we make it the unsuspecting victim of whatever philosophy happens to be prevalent. It seems far more prudent to acknowledge the potential benefit of metaphysics and to ask which metaphysical account coheres with what we find in Scripture" (*Five Things*, 136).

3. At Col 2:8 the NIV rendering "See to it that no one takes you captive through hollow and deceptive philosophy [*tēs philosophias kai kenēs apatēs*]" is superior to the NRSV rendering "See to it that no one takes you captive through philosophy and empty deceit." Because the one article *tēs* governs the two substantives *philosophias* and *kenēs apatēs* (hollow/empty deceit) connected by *kai* (and), the two substantives refer to the same phenomenon ("hollow and deceptive philosophy") rather than two different phenomena (philosophy and empty deceit).

> our proclamation, to save those who believe. For Jews demand signs and Greeks desire wisdom, but we proclaim Christ crucified, a stumbling block to Jews and foolishness to Gentiles, but to those who are the called, both Jews and Greeks, Christ the power of God and the wisdom of God. For God's foolishness is wiser than human wisdom, and God's weakness is stronger than human strength. (1 Cor 1:20–25; see 1 Cor 2:1, 4, 5; 3:19)

Scripture consistently links hollow and deceptive philosophy with pride. Ezekiel thus castigated the king of Tyre: "Your heart was proud because of your beauty; you corrupted your wisdom for the sake of splendor" (Ezek 28:17). In response to some Corinthians' slogan "we all possess knowledge," Paul countered: "But knowledge puffs up while love builds up. Those who think they know something do not yet know as they ought to know. But whoever loves God is known by God" (1 Cor 8:1–3 NIV). The term for "knowledge" in this passage is *gnōsis*, which the Nag Hammadi documents use in referring to secret, esoteric knowledge which is possessed only by the so-called spiritual elite. Paul proceeded in charging Christians to refute arguments based on such knowledge that stand in opposition to God: "We destroy arguments and every proud obstacle raised up against the knowledge of God, and we take every thought captive to obey Christ" (2 Cor 10:4–5).

I suspect that there are myriad differences between genuine philosophical constructs and human-made philosophical constructs. However, I shall focus on those emerging from the data of Scripture and relevant to our purposes. Genuine philosophical constructs do at least one of four things. First, some genuine philosophical constructs cultivate the fruit of the Spirit in those who appreciate them. What James said about the wisdom from above equally applies to some of the constructs that compose such wisdom: they are "first pure, then peaceable, gentle, willing to yield, full of mercy and good fruits, without a trace of partiality or hypocrisy" (Jas 1:17). Second, as the book of Proverbs points out, some genuine philosophical constructs promote the knowledge and fear of God. Along these lines, Paul indicated that the creation of the universe and the universal moral law point to the existence of God (Rom 1:20; 2:14–16). To be sure, cosmological and axiological arguments have proven invaluable in convincing others of God's reality. Third, some genuine philosophical constructs illumine and magnify the being, nature, character, or plan of God. Hence Paul prayed that God would furnish the Ephesian believers "a spirit of wisdom and revelation as you come to know him, so that, with the eyes of your heart enlightened, you may know what is the hope to which he has called you, what are the riches of his glorious inheritance among the saints, and what is the immeasurable greatness of his power for us who believe, according to the working of his great power" (Eph 1:17–19). Fourth, some genuine philosophical concepts clarify the text of Scripture, as seen by the Gospel of John's use of the Logos concept in expanding the account of creation in Genesis 1 (John 1:1–14).

Human-made philosophical constructs do the opposite of one of these four things. Instead of the fruit of the Spirit, some human-made philosophical constructs cultivate pride, arrogance, "envy," "selfish ambition," "disorder," and "wickedness of every kind" in those who appreciate them (Jas 3:14, 16). Second, as Paul observed, some human-made philosophical constructs oppose the knowledge and fear of God (2 Cor 10:4–5). Isaiah described the end result of such constructs among the Babylonians: "You felt secure in your wickedness; you said, 'No one sees me.' Your wisdom and your knowledge led you astray, and you said in your heart, 'I am, and there is no one besides me'" (Isa 47:10). Third, some human-made philosophical constructs obscure and aim to lessen the being, nature, character, or plan of God. This criticism pertains to the philosophical concepts invented by Job's opponents to blame Job for his trials. Fourth, some human-made philosophical constructs muddle the text of Scripture, as witnessed in the last century by Rudolf Bultmann's program of using scientific naturalism plus Martin Heidegger's existentialism to allegedly "demythologize" the text of Scripture.[4]

Upon differentiating these two types of philosophical constructs, it behooves us to use genuine philosophical constructs in biblical interpretation. Jesus called upon us to love God "with all our mind" (Mark 12:30). This includes using truths we learn from other disciplines in our interpretation of Scripture. For all truth is God's truth, and every academic discipline is a ray of light emanating from the one divine source. Such a procedure is uncontroversial regarding the discipline of archaeology. When archaeologists discovered that the term *kataluma* referred to a guest room of a Palestinian home rather than an inn, the NIV Committee on Bible Translation revised Luke 2:7 to read, "She wrapped him in cloths and placed him in a manger, because there was no guest room available for them" (NIV 2011); the NIV 1984 had rendered the second clause as "because there was no room for them in the inn." Likewise, I believe God expects us to use genuine philosophy in biblical interpretation, particularly when its constructs

---

4. Bultmann, *Jesus Christ and Mythology*.

Molinist Philosophical and Theological Ventures

speak directly to an issue raised by the text. For example, several passages of Scripture indicate that God cannot do evil (Ps 5:4; Prov 15:26; Heb 1:13; Jas 1:13; 1 John 1:5; 3 John 11). But other passages of Scripture indicate that God sent evil spirits to people (Judg 9:23; 1 Sam 16:14–15), brought evil on nations (1 Kgs 14:10; 2 Kgs 21:12; Jer 4:6; 11:17; 16:10; 21:10; 24:9; 31:28; 39:16; Mic 2:3), hardened Pharaoh's heart (Exod 4:21; 7:3; 14:4; Rom 9:17–18), and will send a powerful delusion to evildoers in the end times (2 Thess 2:11–12). I take it for granted that Scripture does not contradict itself. Accordingly, it follows that there must be more than one way for God to do or cause something. At this juncture we should use philosophy as theology's handmaiden and ask: Does philosophy include different senses of doing or causing that can make sense of the biblical data? We shall see shortly that it indeed does, and that such senses amplify Scripture and enable believers to consistently maintain the omnibenevolence of God.[5] With this procedure in mind, we now turn to the scriptural information on divine sovereignty, human freedom, predestination, grace, and God's salvific will.

Scriptural Data on Divine Sovereignty

The prophet Daniel exclaimed concerning God: "His kingdom is an everlasting kingdom, and his sovereignty (*sholtān*)[6] is from generation to generation" (Dan 4:3; see also Dan 4:34). The term *sholtān* refers to God's sovereignty in the sense of God's "dominion" or "realm."[7] Likewise, Daniel taught that "the Most High is sovereign (*shalliyt*) over the kingdom of mortals; he gives it to whom he will and sets over it the lowliest of human beings" (Dan 4:17; see also Dan 4:25, 32; 5:21). Having suffered the fate of an insane outcast, Nebuchadnezzar would only be restored to his throne "from the time that you learn that Heaven is sovereign (*shalliyt*)" (Dan 4:26). The term *shalliyt* denotes God's sovereignty in terms of "having" or "exercising . . . mastery," "having authority," and "ruling."[8] Most translations

---

5. Other examples of using genuine philosophical constructs to illuminate Scripture include applying the concepts of *ousia* and *hypostasis* to frame the doctrine of the Trinity and applying the concepts of *hypostasis* and *logos* to frame the doctrine of the two natures of Christ. Most readers will take the Trinity and Christology to be discoveries, not inventions, of human beings that logically follow from the Bible.

6. When transliterating Hebrew, Aramaic, and Greek, I consistently give the lexical form of words instead of their declined or conjugated forms for the sake of convenience.

7. Brown et al., *Hebrew and English Lexicon*, 1115.

8. Brown et al., *Hebrew and English Lexicon*, 1115.

of the Hebrew Bible sometimes (if not always) render the term *'adōnāy* (or *'ādôn*) as "sovereign" when coupled with the divine name Yahweh. To illustrate, Psalm 8:1 is standardly rendered, "O LORD [*Yahweh*], our Sovereign [*'adōnāy*], how majestic is your name in all the earth" (see also Ps 8:9; Isa 1:24; 3:1; 10:16; 10:33; 19:4; 51:22). The term *'adōnāy* (or *'ādôn*) conveys a range of meaning that spans "lord," "master," "superintendent . . . of affairs," "king," "proprietor," "governor," and "Lord of the whole earth."[9] The New Testament also maintains the sovereignty of God. First Timothy 6:15 describes God as "the blessed and only Sovereign [*dynastēs*], the King of kings and Lord of lords." *Dynastēs* connotes "one who is in a position of authority to command others," "ruler."[10] After their arrest by the Sanhedrin, the members of the early Jesus movement prayed to the "sovereign [*despotēs*] Lord, who made the heaven and the earth, the sea, and everything in them" (Acts 4:24). In Revelation the souls of the martyrs cry out to God from beneath the divine altar, "Sovereign [*despotēs*] Lord, holy and true, how long will it be before you judge and avenge our blood on the inhabitants of the earth?" (Rev 6:10). The term *despotēs* conveys two possible shades of meaning. First is "one who holds complete power or authority over another," "master."[11] Second is "one who owns and/or controls the activities of slaves, servants, or subjects, with the implication of absolute, and in some instances, arbitrary jurisdiction," "owner."[12] In the case of God, the jurisdiction God holds would not be arbitrary because he is the creator of all things outside of himself.

From the above instances of biblical terms for "sovereign" and "sovereignty," we develop a robust conception of God's sovereignty, which runs as follows. God owns and has dominion over a realm extending to all created reality. As lord and king, God rules over all created reality, possessing and exercising mastery over it. God therefore superintends and governs all created reality. God possesses total power and authority over the created order. Hence God has the authority to command created beings to carry out God's will. Indeed, God might even control the activities of created beings. This latter point raises two questions. First, to what degree, if any, does God

---

9. Brown et al., *Hebrew and English Lexicon*, 10–11.

10. Louw and Nida, *Greek-English Lexicon*, 1:479; see Bauer et al., *Greek-English Lexicon*, 208.

11. Louw and Nida, *Greek-English Lexicon*, 1:479.

12. Louw and Nida, *Greek-English Lexicon*, 1:559; see Bauer et al., *Greek-English Lexicon*, 176.

Molinist Philosophical and Theological Ventures

control the activities of created beings? Second, if God controls such activities, in what way or ways does God do so?

Regarding the first question, Scripture maintains that God possesses an absolute degree of control over the activities of created beings, including activities that are admittedly random, by chance, or causally unnecessary. Solomon noted concerning choices made by the casting of lots, "The lot is cast into the lap, but the decision is the LORD's alone" (Prov 16:33). The same is true of decisions of earthly rulers: "The king's heart is a stream of water in the hand of the LORD; he turns it wherever he will" (Prov 21:1; see Ezra 1:1; 6:22). Jeremiah ascribed God complete control over mortals, who are unable to guide themselves: "I know, O LORD, that the way of human beings is not in their control, that mortals as they walk cannot direct their steps" (Jer 10:23; see Prov 20:24). Job described God's control over the length of mortals' lives: "their days are determined, and the number of their months is known to you, and you have appointed the bounds that they cannot pass" (Job 14:5). Similarly, Paul remarked on God's control over where and when people live: "From one ancestor he [God] made all nations to inhabit the whole earth, and he allotted the times of their existence and the boundaries of the places where they would live, so that they would search for God and perhaps [*ara*] grope for him and find him" (Acts 17:26–27). Here *ara* "is employed in the context of the tentative, the uncertain, the unresolved, the contingent."[13] Thus people's groping for God and finding God are causally unnecessary. The Bible also describes certain acts occurring randomly, as in the case of Ahab's being shot with an arrow: "But someone drew his bow and randomly [*letummō*] hit the king of Israel between the sections of his armor" (1 Kgs 22:34, my translation; see also 2 Chr 18:33; Prov 26:10).[14] Jesus acknowledged the possibility of chance occurrences in his parable of the Good Samaritan: "Now by chance a priest was going down that road; and when he saw him, he passed by on the other side" (Luke 10:31).[15] Interestingly, the biblical text sees no contradiction between God having an absolute degree of control over something and that thing's potentially happening randomly, by chance, or without causal necessity. The text does not affirm, as many Reformed theologians hold, that because God has an

---

13. Bauer et al., *Greek-English Lexicon*, 104.

14. In support of the accuracy of this translation see Wevers, "First Book of the Kings," 195.

15. In support of the accuracy of this translation see Bauer et al., *Greek-English Lexicon*, 775.

absolute degree of control, nothing happens randomly or by chance. In the aforementioned examples, the text says that God has an absolute degree of control over something and that it happens randomly or by chance!

This fact gives us insight into our second question: God sometimes controls things in such a way that God's control does not remove their contingency. We will find that this concept is especially supported when looking at the next category of biblical passages.

Scriptural Data on Human Freedom

The Bible indicates that humans, even following the events of Genesis 3, possess what philosophers call libertarian human freedom, namely, freedom in at least some circumstances to choose between various alternatives.[16] Nowhere is this clearer than in Moses' exhortation to the Israelites to love God with all their being and to follow Torah.

> Now what I am commanding you today is *not too difficult for you or beyond your reach*. It is not up in heaven, so that you have to ask, "Who will ascend into heaven to get it and proclaim it to us so we may obey it?" Nor is it beyond the sea, so that you have to ask, "Who will cross the sea to get it and proclaim it to us so we may obey it?" No, the word is very near you; it is in your mouth and in your heart *so you may obey it*. See, I set before you today life and prosperity, death and destruction. For I command you today to love the LORD your God, to walk in obedience to him, and to keep his commands, decrees, and laws; then you will live and increase, and the LORD your God will bless you in the land you are entering to possess. But if your heart turns away and you are not obedient, and if you are drawn away to bow down to other gods and worship them, I declare to you this day that you will certainly be destroyed. You will not live long in the land you are crossing the Jordan to enter and possess. This day I call the heavens and the

---

16. This understanding of libertarian freedom defeats so-called Frankfurt-style counterexamples to the principle of alternate possibilities. Such counterexamples feature situations like the following. In the 2020 US presidential election, a mad scientist and fervent Trump supporter implants into my brain, unbeknownst to me, an electrical device. Once I step into the polling booth, this device forces my hands and fingers to register a vote for Trump if I choose to vote for Biden (or for some other candidate or for no one at all) but exerts no causal pressure on me if I choose to vote for Trump. In any case, I cannot do otherwise but vote for Trump. However, libertarian freedom (and the principle of alternate possibilities) still stands because I retain the power to choose to vote for Biden or for Trump (or for some other candidate or for no one at all).

earth as witnesses against you that I have set before you life and death, blessings and curses. Now choose life, so that you and your children may live. (Deut 30:11–19 NIV, emphasis added)

Among Hebrew Bible scholars, the translation of the italicized words is not in dispute. They rule out the suggestion of Martin Luther and John Calvin that Moses was telling the Israelites what they should do but lacked the ability to do in order to reveal to them the depth of their sinfulness.[17] For the italicized words explicitly reveal that the Israelites had the ability to choose to love God maximally and follow Torah: doing so was "not too difficult for them or beyond their reach," and the command was in their mouth and heart precisely so that they "may obey it." This ability extends to the matter of salvation (choosing whether or not to love God with all one's being) and is not merely limited to mundane affairs. We know from Deuteronomy and Joshua that many of these Israelites were unregenerate. However, the passage does not answer the question of the source of this ability, which we shall discuss later in the section on grace.

In his discussion of temptation, Paul affirmed that Christian believers possess libertarian freedom: "No temptation has overtaken you except what is common to mankind. And God is faithful; he will not let you be tempted beyond what you can bear. But when you are tempted, he will also provide a way out so that *you can endure it*" (1 Cor 10:13 NIV, emphasis added). The translation of the italicized words is uncontested among New Testament scholars—the verb translated "you can" is *dunasthai*, which may equally well be rendered "you are able to." So the believer, amidst temptation, has the ability to take the way out God gives or to succumb to the temptation.[18] These two passages show that, for unbeliever and believer alike, when God commands someone to do something, the familiar logical and legal principle applies—ought implies can. Hence Moses presented the Israelites with two live options when he said, "See, I am setting before you today a blessing and a curse: the blessing, if you obey the commandments of the Lord your God that I am commanding you today; and the curse, if you do not obey the commandments of the Lord your God, but turn from the way that I am commanding you today, to follow other gods that you have not known" (Deut 11:26–28).

---

17. Luther, *Freedom of a Christian*, 57; Calvin, *Institutes* 2.5.7; 2.8.3.
18. Stratton, *Freedom, Knowledge, and Molinism*, 180–82.

Likewise, God's announcement of hating the condemnation of evil persons and consequent imploring of the Israelites, upon their unfaithfulness, to repent of their sins and find salvation were sincere:

> Have I any pleasure in the death of the wicked, says the Lord God, and not rather that they should turn from their ways and live? . . . Repent and turn from all your transgressions; otherwise iniquity will be your ruin. Cast away from you all the transgressions that you have committed against me, and get yourselves a new heart and a new spirit! Why will you die, O house of Israel? For I have no pleasure in the death in anyone, says the Lord God. Turn, then, and live. (Ezek 18:23, 30–32; see also Ezek 33:11; Isa 55:1–3, 6–7)

Notice God's command for the Israelites to get themselves a new heart and a new spirit, which God also says he will give the Israelites: "I will give you a new heart and put a new spirit in you; I will remove from you your heart of stone and give you a heart of flesh. And I will put my Spirit in you and move you to follow my decrees and be careful to keep my laws" (Ezek 36:26–27 NIV). This leads us to raise the question: how can both divine statements be true? Although not reaching the same conclusion he does, I resonate with the following clue furnished by Wayne Grudem: "it is possible to affirm that in one sense events are fully (100 percent) caused by God and fully (100 percent) caused by the creature as well. However, divine and creaturely causes work in different ways."[19] While affirming that God controls all things, the Bible simultaneously affirms that God does so in such a way to allow for human freedom.

This affirmation is echoed in the words of Jesus. Jesus presented all persons with two live options when he famously remarked: "For God so loved the world [*kosmos*] that he gave his only Son, so that everyone who believes in him may not perish but may have eternal life. Indeed, God did not send the Son into the world [*kosmos*] to condemn the world [*kosmos*], but in order that the world [*kosmos*] may be saved through him" (John 3:16–17). As I have argued elsewhere, "The Father loves ὁ κόσμος [*ho kosmos*], namely the physical planet and the people therein . . . as opposed to simply some of the people therein. All people are given the opportunity to pledge their allegiance to Jesus and so gain eternal life. The Father has no desire to judge ὁ κόσμος [*ho kosmos*] but desires that every person will be

---

19. Grudem, *Systematic Theology*, 319.

Molinist Philosophical and Theological Ventures

saved through Jesus."[20] Jesus reiterated the choice between eternal life and eternal death in the Sermon on the Mount:

> Everyone then who hears these words of mine and acts on them will be like a wise man who built his house on rock. The rain fell, the floods came, and the winds blew and beat on that house, but it did not fall, because it had been founded on rock. And everyone who hears these words of mine and does not act on them will be like a foolish man who built his house on sand. The rain fell, and the floods came, and the winds blew and beat against that house, and it fell—and great was its fall. (Matt 7:24–27)

Similarly, John the Baptist delineated the decision facing all human beings: "Whoever believes in the Son has eternal life; whoever disobeys the Son will not see life, but must endure God's wrath" (John 3:36). That the gospel offer of eternal life is open to everyone is entailed by the Great Commission, as Jesus commanded his apostles to "go therefore and make disciples of all the nations . . . teaching them to obey everything that I have commanded you" (Matt 28:19–20). The biblical nature of "ought implies can" indicates that all persons have the ability to obey Jesus' aforementioned statements and receive salvation.

Often Reformed theologians object to this conclusion on the grounds that unregenerate humans are spiritually dead, a notion they equate with the lack of libertarian freedom.[21] It is true that Paul described unregenerate humans as "dead through the trespasses and sins in which you once lived" (Eph 2:1–2; see also Eph 2:5) and "by nature children of wrath, like everyone else" (Eph 2:3). However, no good grounds can be given for equating spiritual death with the lack of libertarian freedom. Rather, spiritual death means spiritual separation from God, or lack of relational union with God:

> In Scripture the concept of an entity's death spells not its extinction but its separation from the immaterial reality without which it lacks meaningful existence. Hence a human's death denotes the separation of the body from its vivifying soul; by the same token, spiritual death, namely the death of a finite spirit or soul, signifies the separation of that finite spirit from the Infinite Spirit, the Trinitarian God, with which that finite spirit requires union if not to succumb to the existential threat of absurdity. So when Paul asserts that unregenerate humanity is spiritually dead or dead "in

---

20. MacGregor, *John's Gospel*, 150.
21. This equation was first made by Calvin, *Institutes* 2.2.1–10.

transgressions and sins" (Eph. 2:1), he means that their spirits are alienated from the Divine Spirit and thereby relegated to lives of pointlessness; this is why Paul interchanges phrases connoting spiritual death with such descriptive phrases as "separate from Christ," "without hope and without God in the world" (2:12), "living in the futility of their thinking" (3:17), and "darkened in their understanding and separated from the life of God" (3:18).[22]

It could now be alleged that a human body physically separated from a soul cannot do anything; likewise, a soul spiritually separated from God cannot do anything. However, that would be to overlook a crucial difference between a human body and a human soul: a human body is naturally mortal, while a human soul is naturally immortal.[23] For a soul is immaterial and therefore indestructible upon its creation.[24] Unlike the body, the soul continues to exist even without relational union with God.[25] This fact is obvious when we consider that the souls of unregenerate persons function, as such persons possess memory, will, reason, consciousness, thoughts, beliefs, desires, sensations, and self-identity over time, all of which are faculties of the soul, not the body.[26] So the souls of unregenerate persons clearly cannot be compared with corpses in a graveyard. Now as J. P. Moreland has argued, libertarian freedom is also a function of the soul. For if human beings could be reduced to their brains and the rest of their bodies, then everything that they do would be determined by their genetic makeup and the input of their five senses.[27] But this is obviously false; an unregenerate person's soul can resist the impulses of the brain and act contrary to its messages. Any unregenerate person who goes on a diet, stops smoking, or successfully liberates oneself from a neuropsychological anxiety disorder

22. MacGregor, *Systematic Theology*, 25–26.

23. As John Walton has demonstrated, humankind was created mortal. This fact is entailed by Adam, archetypally representing the entire human race, being formed from dust (Gen 2:7; Ps 103:14), which equals mortality (Gen 3:19). It is further entailed by Adam and Eve's needing to eat from a tree of life to remain alive (Gen 2:9; 3:22–24), which immortal people would not need; a tree of life is the antidote to our natural condition of mortality (Walton, *Adam and Eve*, 72–77).

24. Annihilationists disagree with me here, holding that the soul is conditionally immortal upon faith in Christ.

25. However, nothing can exist without the sustaining or repletive presence of God, which is everywhere in the universe and even in hell. So even naturally immortal entities like the soul could not continue to exist apart from God's repletive presence.

26. Moreland delineates some of these in *Soul*, 132–39, 149–50.

27. Moreland, *Soul*, 128–32.

like OCD is testimony to that fact. It would be contrary to the evidence, not to mention arbitrary, to contend that the souls of unregenerate persons possess every faculty that souls of regenerate persons possess except libertarian freedom.

Philosophical Reflections on Divine Sovereignty and Human Freedom

In view of libertarian human freedom, does philosophy shed any light on how God could control all things without removing such freedom and contingency in general? Indeed it does: control can be achieved by either strong actualization or weak actualization. Strong actualization means directly causing something to happen. In this case, the actualizer is morally responsible for the effect. Weak actualization means indirectly causing something to happen by creating circumstances in which a third party directly causes something to happen.[28] If the actions of the third party are not intended by the actualizer even if foreseeable to the actualizer, and if the actualizer creates the circumstances for some good reason standing contrary to the third party's actions, then the actualizer is not morally responsible for the effect of the third party.[29] On the contrary, if the actions of the third party are intended by the actualizer, then the actualizer bears some moral responsibility for the effect of the third party. I illustrate with the following example. Imagine that a professor announced to his class that he would sit in his office during that day's exam for the good purpose of allowing his class to take personal responsibility for the Student Integrity Code and manifest their academic honesty while un-proctored. However, the professor knew his students so well that he realized one of them would cheat if he were to leave the exam un-proctored. As I have explained elsewhere, "Obviously the student is morally responsible for the cheating, and the teacher bears no moral responsibility for the cheating. Nevertheless, the teacher did weakly [actualize] the cheating by placing the student in circumstances where, despite the teacher's intentions to the contrary, the student freely chose to cheat."[30]

---

28. MacGregor, *Molina*, 109.

29. This follows from the Doctrine of Double Effect (DDE), explained by Shafer-Landau, *Ethics*, 219.

30. MacGregor, *Molina*, 109.

Likewise, God may create various circumstances for the good purpose (among several) of allowing human freedom, willing that humans always use it to do the right thing and avoid sin. However, Scripture teaches that God possesses foreknowledge of hypothetical conditionals, or conditionals in the subjunctive mood (i.e., if such-and-such were the case, then so-and-so would be the case). Hence God foreknows, for any possible person and set of circumstances, how the person would respond if s/he were in that set of circumstances (as evidenced in 1 Sam 23:9–13; Jer 38:17–18; Matt 11:20–24; Luke 10:13–15; John 15:22–24; 18:36; 1 Cor 2:8).[31] So God knows in advance the sins that people would commit were he to place them in various circumstances, sins that are unwanted side-effects of placing them in those circumstances. In that case, humans bear sole moral responsibility for their own sins, with God exempted from any such responsibility. God "does not willingly afflict or grieve anyone" (Lam 3:33). God bears some moral responsibility for good human actions, and God bears complete moral responsibility for actions that he directly actualizes. As the greatest conceivable being, God only directly actualizes good things. Consequently, God is totally or partially responsible for all good that occurs in the world and is not responsible for any evil that occurs in the world. Yet God still controls all things, via either strong or weak actualization. This makes sense of passages such as the following: "The plans of the mind belong to mortals, but the answer of the tongue is from the LORD" (Prov 16:1). Or again, "the human mind plans the way, but the LORD directs the steps" (Prov 16:9). By placing mortals in circumstances, knowing in advance the words and actions they would freely take were he to do so, God controls the events via weak actualization and mortals control the events via strong actualization. But now the question arises: when evil occurs as an unwanted side-effect, how does God respond to that evil?

In his omniscience and omnibenevolence, God responds to each evil by bringing good out of it for those who love him and thus furthering his will. As Scripture testifies: "And we know that to those loving God, he works all things together for good, to those being called according to his purpose" (Rom 8:28, my translation). Likewise, "in him [Christ] we were also chosen, having been predestined according to the plan of him who works out everything in conformity with the purpose of his will" (Eph 1:11 NIV). Notice that God is not a consequentialist, operating according to the principle that the ends justify the means. God does not intend any

---

31. I exposit these biblical passages in MacGregor, *Molina*, 80–84.

evil—period—much less that good may result from it.³² Both Romans 8:28 and Ephesians 1:11

> are *a posteriori*, not *a priori*, portrayals of God's operation upon "all things"; in other words, they take as given the previous existence of "all things" and simply describe what God then does with these things, namely, working them together for the good of believers and for the purpose of his will. These texts do not state that God performs, ordains, or purposes all things for either the accomplishment of believers' benefit or his will; instead, they depict God as confronted with certain already performed events . . . many of which . . . are positively contrary to and outside of his will, and assure us of God's power and intelligence to take even these events and use them for our and ultimately his benefit.³³

Moreover, God does not need evil to bring about any good. If some evil had not occurred, then God would bring about the same good or an even greater good for those who love him through purely righteous means.³⁴ However, given that an evil has occurred as an unwanted side-effect of divinely created circumstances, God could either use that evil to bring about good or to simply do nothing at all with it. Obviously, it is morally better to do the former than the latter. God, then, is the ultimate follower of the biblical maxim, "Do not be overcome by evil, but overcome evil with good" (Rom 12:21).

Let me provide two classic examples of this point, which constitutes the hallmark of God's providence. First, Joseph's brothers committed the unspeakable evils of capturing Joseph (Gen 37:23–24), selling him into slavery (Gen 37:25–28), and deceiving their father Jacob into believing that Joseph had been killed by a wild animal (Gen 37:31–33). Potiphar's wife committed the sin of falsely accusing Joseph of rape (Gen 39:14–18), which led Potiphar to unjustly have Joseph thrown into prison (Gen 39:20). After Joseph correctly interpreted the cupbearer's dream (Gen 40:9–15, 20–21), the cupbearer forgot to tell Pharaoh about Joseph's situation (Gen 40:23). God did not will for any of these events to happen; the responsibility for each one lies entirely with the human agent or agents. These events were weakly, not strongly, actualized by God. Yet God chose, in his infinite wisdom, to use these wrongs for the good purpose of saving the lives of many

---

32. MacGregor, "Gratuitous Evil," 169–71.
33. MacGregor, "Gratuitous Evil," 170.
34. MacGregor, "Gratuitous Evil," 171.

people in the Ancient Near East. As Joseph commented to his brothers, "Even though you intended to do harm to me, God intended it for good, in order to preserve a numerous people, as he is doing today" (Gen 50:20).[35] Second, consider the monstrous evil of Jesus' crucifixion. This event was brought about by the Sanhedrin's plotting to take Jesus' life (John 11:47–53), Judas' betraying Jesus for thirty pieces of silver (Matt 22:14–16; 26:47–49; Mark 14:10–11, 43–46; Luke 22:3–6, 47–48; John 18:2–3), the Sanhedrin falsely convicting Jesus for blasphemy and turning him over to Pilate as a rebel king (Matt 26:65–66; 27:1–2; Mark 14:63–65; 15:1; Luke 22:71—23:2; John 18:28–32), and Pilate's unjust sentencing of Jesus to be crucified for the sake of Pilate's own self-preservation (John 19:12–16) despite knowing that Jesus was not, in fact, a violent revolutionary (John 18:33–38). Each of these were atrocious sins which God did not will and concerning whose perpetrators Jesus begged, "Father, forgive them; for they do not know what they are doing" (Luke 23:34). However, God amazingly chose to use Jesus' crucifixion to reconcile the world to himself (2 Cor 5:18–21). Because God willed to weakly actualize the aforementioned events and strongly actualize Jesus' resurrection, Peter stated on the day of Pentecost, "This man, handed over to you according to the definite plan and foreknowledge of God, you crucified and killed by the hands of those outside the law. But God raised him up, having freed him from death, because it was impossible for him to be held in its power" (Acts 2:23–24; see also Acts 4:27–28). All of this was in accord with God's foreknowledge, in that God knew what would happen in the relevant circumstances, and God's plan, which includes everything that God actualizes either strongly or weakly.[36]

Conclusion to Part One

Shining the light of genuine philosophy upon Scripture explains how God can control free human decisions and other contingent events: he weakly actualizes them rather than strongly actualizing them. In other words, God creates the circumstances in which the free decisions and contingent events occur, knowing in advance of creating such circumstances the free decisions and contingent events that would occur therein. God creates every set of circumstances for some good purpose, never doing so in order that evil would occur. However, if divinely unintended evil occurs, God exhibits his brilliant

---

35. Craig, "Middle-Knowledge Response," 58; MacGregor, *Molina*, 113.
36. Craig, "Middle-Knowledge View," 134–35; MacGregor, *Molina*, 113.

ability and intelligence by using it for the advancement of his own good will (without needing it to advance his will) and for the good of believers.

When Scripture claims that God causes good things, God does so either by strong actualization or by weak actualization. If God directly does the good, such as creating the universe, parting the Red Sea, becoming incarnate as Jesus of Nazareth, forgiving someone's sin, and so forth, then God strongly actualizes the good. If humans directly do the good in circumstances created by God, then God weakly actualizes the good. When Scripture claims that God causes evil things, such as sending evil spirits to people, bringing evil on nations, hardening Pharaoh's heart, and sending a powerful delusion to evildoers in the end times, God does so by weak actualization. God sent evil spirits to people in the sense that God created circumstances for good purposes in which evil spirits afflicted people as unintended, yet foreknown, consequences. The same is true of God bringing evil on nations. God hardened Pharaoh's heart by creating circumstances for good purposes in which Pharaoh freely hardened his own heart, a divinely unwanted side-effect God knew in advance. God will send a powerful delusion to end-time evildoers when he creates circumstances for good purposes in which he foreknows that, tragically, end-time evildoers would believe a strong delusion. And when the aforementioned evils occur, God does not let them "sit there" but conquers them by ingeniously working good from them.[37]

---

37. MacGregor, *Molina*, 114–15.

— 2 —

Molinism and the Bible

Part Two

HAVING SEEN HOW THE distinction between strong actualization and weak actualization enables us to reconcile the biblical data on divine sovereignty and human freedom, we now turn to the biblical data on predestination, grace, and God's universal salvific will. We shall continue to use philosophy as a handmaiden to theology by availing ourselves of its insights when the biblical data raises unanswered questions. By the end of this chapter, we will see how the Molinist structure logically emerges from this procedure.

Scriptural Data on Predestination

It is undeniably true that Scripture affirms the fact of persons being predestined to salvation. Three representative examples will suffice. Paul wrote: "For he [the Father] chose us in him [Christ] before the creation of the world to be holy and blameless in his sight. In love he predestined us for adoption to sonship through Jesus Christ, in accordance with his pleasure and will" (Eph 1:4–5 NIV; see also 1 Thess 1:4; 2 Thess 2:13). Luke affirmed regarding new converts' listening to the gospel message: "When the Gentiles heard this, they were glad and praised the word of the Lord; and as many as had been destined for eternal life became believers" (Acts 13:48). Finally, Jesus declared: "All things have been handed over to me by my Father; and no one knows the Son except the Father, and no one knows the Father except the Son *and anyone to whom the Son chooses to reveal him*" (Matt 11:27, emphasis added; see also Luke 10:22). Nevertheless, the most famous text on predestination is Romans 9. There are two competing paradigms claiming to be the proper interpretive lens for its interpretation. First is the intertextual Jewish paradigm, which claims that Paul in his citations of the Hebrew Bible uses metalepsis, or allusion "to . . . earlier text in a way that evokes resonances of the earlier text *beyond those explicitly cited*,"[1] to prove that God has sovereignly chosen to predicate membership in the covenant community on faith, thus including Gentiles who believe in Jesus, rather than works of Torah and lineage from Abraham, thus precluding Jews who do not believe in Jesus.[2] Second is the Augustinian-Calvinistic paradigm, which claims that Paul is intending to teach sovereign individual predestination of specific individuals to eternal salvation or eternal condemnation, using only the portions of the Hebrew Bible he explicitly cites. As a historian, I am persuaded by the intertextual Jewish paradigm. Accordingly, I doubt that the text is really about predestination of individuals. However, I wish *arguendo* to assume the accuracy of the Augustinian-Calvinistic paradigm, which, coincidentally, Luis de Molina also assumed.[3]

The first passage in Romans mentioning predestination is 8:29–30: "For those whom he foreknew he also predestined to be conformed to the image of his Son, in order that he might be the firstborn within a large family. And those whom he predestined he also called; and those whom he called he also justified; and those whom he justified he also glorified." Notice that the passage renders predestination logically posterior to foreknowledge (noun form *prognōsis*; verb form *proginōskō*), which literally means "to know beforehand." The opening of 1 Peter makes the same predication: "To God's elect . . . who have been chosen according to the foreknowledge of God the Father" (1 Pet 1:1–2 NIV).[4] Such knowledge could either be

---

1. Hays, *Conversion*, 2.

2. Abasciano, *Romans 9.1–9*; Abasciano, *Romans 9.10–18*; Abasciano, "Corporate Election."

3. MacGregor, *Molina*, 135–57.

4. As William Lane Craig points out regarding Romans 8:29–30 and 1 Peter 1:1–2, "Here the meaning of 'foreknow' cannot be reduced without redundancy to 'foreordain,' since Peter has already referred to his readers as chosen or elect, while Paul uses 'foreordain' as a consequence of 'foreknow.' It is sometimes suggested that 'foreknow' with regard to the elect means 'choose in advance,' so that foreknowledge and unconditional election to salvation become synonymous. But . . . there is no linguistic evidence in support of this suggestion. Out of the 770 cases of *yāda'* ('to know') in the Old Testament, the 660 instances of *ginōskō* ('to know') in the Septuagint, and the 220 in the New Testament, the term never carries the sense of 'choose' or 'elect'" (*Only Wise God*, 34).

prior knowledge of facts *simpliciter* or prior relational knowledge, as suggested by the Hebrew Bible verb *yāda'*. However, prior relational knowledge of someone entails prior knowledge of facts about someone: "For if God had prior relational knowledge of the persons whom he would predestine before those persons existed, that relational knowledge would technically be of their individual essences, which existed as ideas in the mind of God. And full relational knowledge of someone's individual essence would encompass knowing everything that individual essence, if instantiated, would freely do under any set of circumstances."[5] However, Romans 9, on the Augustinian-Calvinistic paradigm, maintains that predestination is not based upon prior knowledge of works of any kind or even faith. Referring to God's choice of Jacob over Esau, the chapter explains:

> Even before they had been born or had done anything good or bad (so that God's purpose of election might continue, not by works but by his call) she was told, "The elder shall serve the younger." As it is written, "I have loved Jacob, but I have hated Esau." What then are we to say? Is there injustice on God's part? By no means! For he says to Moses, "I will have mercy on whom I have mercy, and I will have compassion on whom I have compassion." So it depends not on human will or exertion, but on God who shows mercy. For the scripture says to Pharaoh, "I have raised you up for the very purpose of showing my power in you, so that my name may be proclaimed in all the earth." So then he has mercy on whomever he chooses, and he hardens the heart of whomever he chooses. (Rom 9:11–18)

Piecing together Romans 8:29–30 (and 1 Peter 1:1–2) with Romans 9:11–18, we reach the conclusion that predestination is *both* in accordance with *and* not based upon foreknowledge of prior facts about those chosen for salvation (elected) or those chosen for condemnation (reprobated).[6] And Paul insisted that this situation is not unjust. In support of this insistence, we

---

5. MacGregor, *Molina*, 143.

6. An important question is whether reprobation implies eternity in hell, the annihilation of the soul, or a less than eternal period in hell culminating in salvation. This is the debate between traditionalists, annihilationists, and what I shall dub eventual universalists. By eventual universalism I mean the position that hell exists and that the lost go to hell but eventually learn from the error of their ways and turn to God, whereupon God ultimately gives them eternal life. Eventual universalism is the position taken by evangelical universalists like Talbott, *Inescapable Love*; Parry, *Evangelical Universalist*. While I am a traditionalist myself, I think a Molinist could hold to annihilationism or eventual universalism. I discuss eventual universalism in chapter 8.

recall our observation in chapter 1 that God hardens people's hearts by creating circumstances for good purposes in which those people freely harden their own hearts as divinely unwanted side-effects known in advance. We shall see later how philosophical analysis illuminates this situation.

Paul then raised the potential objection: "One of you will say to me: 'Then why does God still blame us? For who is able to resist his will?'" (Rom 9:19 NIV). The question assumes, illicitly as we saw in chapter 1, that God's will is irresistible, which would deny human freedom. Paul responded to the objection in two ways. First, Paul asked the ironic question: "But who are you, a human being, to talk back to God?" (Rom 9:20 NIV). Obviously talking back to God is against God's will! Paul supported this fact with his citation of Isaiah 29:16 and 45:9, "Shall what is formed say to the one who formed it, 'Why did you make me like this?'" (Rom 9:20 NIV)—a question whose answer is no. The imagined interlocutor has thus proven, by asking his question, that he has the power to resist God's will and is blameworthy for doing so, thus rendering his objection self-refuting. With the datum of human freedom on the table, Paul secondly argued that God, like a potter, bears the prerogative of bestowing glory upon some members of his creation and displaying wrath against other members of his creation:

> Does not the potter have the right to make out of the same lump of clay some pottery for special purposes and some for common use? What if God, although choosing to show his wrath and make his power known, bore with great patience the objects of his wrath—prepared for destruction? What if he did this to make the riches of his glory known to the objects of his mercy, whom he prepared in advance for glory—even us, whom he also called, not only from the Jews but also from the Gentiles? (Rom 9:19–24 NIV)

Shedding special light on this passage is Ephesians 2:3–5, which indicates that all persons were once objects of God's wrath but that God chooses to graciously render some objects of mercy: "All of us once lived among them [the disobedient] in the passions of our flesh, following the desires of flesh and senses, and we were by nature children of wrath, like everyone else. But God, who is rich in mercy, out of the great love with which he loved us even when we were dead through our trespasses, made us alive together with Christ—by grace you have been saved." Hence a person can go from being a vessel of wrath to being a vessel of mercy.

One could argue that John 6 teaches sovereign individual predestination of specific persons to salvation or condemnation. I am inclined to think it does, and I have addressed elsewhere how the inability described by the statement "No one can come to me unless drawn by the Father who sent me; and I will raise that person up on the last day" (John 6:44; see also 6:65) is different from and harmonious with the ability that persons possess to choose for or against loving God.[7] However, John 6 could also be seen as having nothing to do with sovereign individual predestination. Immediately after the aforementioned statement, Jesus continued: "It is written in the prophets: 'And they shall all be taught by God.' Everyone who has heard and learned from the Father comes to me" (John 6:45). If John 6:45 explains the meaning of Jesus' terms in John 6:44, then being drawn by the Father indicates having heard and learned from the Father, which our discussion of human freedom reveals anyone is able to do. When someone hears and learns from the Father's teaching, the Father, in the calculus of salvation, grants that person the ability of coming to (i.e., receiving salvation from) Jesus (John 6:65) and gives that person to Jesus (John 6:37). Since Jesus speaks the Father's words, such that whoever has seen Jesus has seen the Father (John 14:8–10), one can hear and learn from the Father by hearing and learning from Jesus. At this logical moment, the Father enables the person to receive salvation from and belong to Jesus.

Scriptural Data on Grace

In contrast to Eastern Orthodoxy, Roman Catholic and Protestant forms of Christianity have typically held to the doctrine of original sin. The strongest form of original sin is found in the Augustinian-Calvinist tradition, which holds that primal humanity, in rebelling against God, destroyed not only their but also their descendants' mental ability to do anything spiritually good, or good in the sight of God.[8] Even if libertarian freedom is an essential faculty of the soul, proponents of this tradition argue that such freedom would then exist but that its scope, in Luther's terminology, is now limited to matters below and does not extend to matters above.[9] Coming out of an Anabaptist tradition, I have grave reservations about the doctrine

---

7. MacGregor, *John's Gospel*, 145–57.

8. Augustine, *Enchiridion* 9.30; Augustine, *Against Julian* 2.8.23; Augustine, *Perfection in Righteousness* 4.9; Augustine, *Against Two Letters* 3.8.24; Augustine, *Letters* 145.2; Calvin, *Institutes* 2.1.7–9; 2.2.1, 8. The Augustine citations are taken from Battles and McNeill's footnotes to Calvin, *Institutes* 2.2.8 (1:265nn39, 41–43).

9. Luther, *Bondage of the Will*, 189–90.

Molinist Philosophical and Theological Ventures

of original sin, as it does not seem to me supported by the opening chapters of Genesis.[10] However, I shall suppose for the sake of argument that the Augustinian-Calvinist form of original sin is correct. The only way it could be reconciled with the other scriptural *loci* we have examined is if there is some way that God has supernaturally restored to fallen humanity the mental faculty to do spiritual good and thus the full scope of libertarian freedom, extending to matters above. There exists biblical reason to suppose that God has done exactly this through his grace.

Titus 2:11 remarks: "For the grace of God has appeared, bringing salvation to all." To avoid the potential implication that everyone is forced to accept this salvation, the NIV translates the verse, "For the grace of God has appeared that offers salvation to all people." Hence divine grace makes salvation choose-able to every person, which logically entails that grace has remedied any spiritual defect prohibiting this choice.[11] Paul made the same point in Romans 5:12–21. Contrasting the sin of Adam with the death of Jesus, Paul explained: "Therefore just as one man's trespass led to condemnation for all, so one man's act of righteousness leads to justification and life for all. For just as by the one man's disobedience the many were made sinners, so by the one man's obedience the many will be made righteous" (Rom 5:18–19). In my judgment, this text teaches that Jesus' death facilitates the potential salvation of all.[12] It therefore implies that everyone is able to choose whether to appropriate salvation, a choice rooted in the grace of the Father and the Son: "For if the many died through the one man's trespass, much more surely have the grace of God and the free gift in the grace of the one man, Jesus Christ, abounded to the many" (Rom 5:15). The interchangeability of "many" and "all" in Romans 5:12–21 guarantees that "many" in 5:15 means "all."

Several passages of Scripture speak of an enlightening that God gives to all people. Referring to Jesus, John 1:9 observes: "The true light,

---

10. MacGregor, *Systematic Theology*, 20–24. Referring among other doctrines to original sin, the Hebrew Bible scholar John Collins writes concerning Genesis 1–3, "More than most stories, these chapters of Genesis have been overlaid with theological interpretations that have little basis in the Hebrew text" (*Hebrew Bible*, 40).

11. See further discussion of this verse in Shelton, *Prevenient Grace*, 54–56.

12. Eventual universalists disagree and hold that Jesus' death facilitates the eventual salvation of all (notwithstanding the reality of hell). For the exposition of the eventual universalist interpretation see Talbott, *Inescapable Love*, 51–58; Parry, *Evangelical Universalist*, 78–84. For the exposition of the interpretation I hold see Harrison, "Romans," 60–65; Wright, "Romans," 522–32.

which enlightens everyone, was coming into the world." W. Brian Shelton effectively argues that "this light metaphor describes the opportunity of salvation for humankind living in a fallen world of darkness."[13] The same point is made in John 8:12, where Jesus stated: "I am the light of the world (*kosmos*). Whoever follows me will never walk in darkness but will have the light of life."[14] Recall from chapter 1 that *kosmos* includes every person without exception. The universality of the light is also depicted in Proverbs 29:13: "The poor and the oppressor have this in common: the LORD gives light to the eyes of both." Shelton comments: "Solomon here recognizes a divine 'enlightening' that enables all people to live in righteousness. Both the oppressor and the oppressed are created and provided for by God . . . 'God enlightens both poor and oppressor' indiscriminately, so that each can live the life of wisdom for which Proverbs calls. This wisdom is the way of righteousness (Prov 15:9) and the path of light (Prov 4:18) that leads to both prosperity and eternal life."[15] Accordingly, the light God gives everyone includes the ability to appropriate salvation.

Regardless of whether one sees the Father's drawing as pertaining to individual predestination in John 6, Jesus' description of the effect of his impending crucifixion is clearly salvific: "And I, when I am lifted up from the earth, will draw all people to myself" (John 12:32). Since all people do not seem to be saved, the passage must mean that Jesus grants the opportunity for salvation to all people through his death.[16] This gracious bestowal is also portrayed by Paul in terms of divine kindness: "Do you not realize that God's kindness is meant to lead you to repentance?" (Rom 2:4). Since this kindness is given to everyone, Jew and Gentile alike, all have the ability to repent.[17] Consequently, God justly—namely, impartially—judges each person based on whether they availed themselves of the opportunity to repent:

> For he will repay according to each one's deeds: to those who by patiently doing good seek for glory and honor and immortality, he will give eternal life; while for those who are self-seeking and who obey not the truth but wickedness, there will be wrath and fury. There will be anguish and distress for everyone who does evil, the

---

13. Shelton, *Prevenient Grace*, 24.

14. Shelton, *Prevenient Grace*, 24.

15. Shelton, *Prevenient Grace*, 31.

16. See further discussion of this and other verses on drawing in Shelton, *Prevenient Grace*, 39–47.

17. See further discussion of Romans 2:4 in Shelton, *Prevenient Grace*, 47–51.

Jew first and also the Greek, but glory and honor and peace for everyone who does good, the Jew first and also the Greek. For God shows no partiality. (Rom 2:6–11)

The divine grace, enlightening, drawing by Jesus, and kindness discussed in this section has been encapsulated historically under the term "prevenient grace."[18]

Scriptural Data on God's Universal Salvific Will

Perhaps paradoxically in view of predestination, the Bible explicitly teaches that God wills for each person he creates to find salvation. Paul portrayed "God our Savior" as one "who desires everyone to be saved and to come to the knowledge of the truth" (1 Tim 2:3–4). In response to the question of why Jesus' second coming had not already happened, Peter explained: "The Lord is not slow about his promise, as some think of slowness, but is patient with you, not wanting any to perish, but all to come to repentance" (2 Pet 3:9). Hence the second coming is divinely delayed to furnish people more time to turn from their sins and embrace God. On the same score, recall from chapter 1 God's pleas in the book of Ezekiel for the wicked to turn from their ways, as God does not desire the destruction of anyone (Ezek 18:23, 30–32; see also Ezek 33:11). John the Elder explained to the Christian community in Ephesus that "Jesus Christ the righteous . . . is the atoning sacrifice for our sins, and not for ours only but also for the sins of the *whole world* (*holos kosmos*)" (1 John 2:1–2, emphasis added). This passage claims that the divine intent of Jesus' death was not merely to make atonement for the sins of believers but also to make atonement for the sins of every non-believer—a point emphasized by appending "whole" (*holos*) to "world" (*kosmos*). This intent would be evacuated of any substance if God did not also will for every non-believer to avail themselves of Christ's atonement.

Moreover, God's universal salvific will is implied in a number of other biblical passages. The New Testament teaches that discipleship or allegiance to Jesus as Lord, i.e., faith, is divinely reckoned to a person as righteousness, thereby procuring their salvation (Rom 4; Gal 3:6–9).[19] In the Great Commission Jesus declared: "Go therefore and make disciples of all the nations"

---

18. See Shelton, *Prevenient Grace*, 1–11, 59–98.
19. See Bates, *Salvation by Allegiance Alone*.

(Matt 28:19; see also Isa 49:6). This entails that Jesus wanted all the nations to be saved. Describing the relationship between Jews and Gentiles, Paul wrote:

> Just as you [believing Gentiles] who were at one time disobedient to God have now received mercy as a result of their [non-believing Jews'] disobedience, so too they [non-believing Jews] have now become disobedient in order that they too may now receive mercy as a result of God's mercy to you [believing Gentiles]. For God has bound everyone over to disobedience so that he may have mercy on them all. (Rom 11:30–32 NIV)

The significant part of this text for our purposes is that God desires to have mercy, which in the context of Romans 11 is salvific mercy (vv. 11–12, 25–26), on all, whether Jew or Gentile. The same sentiment is conveyed by David: "The Lord is good to all, and his compassion is over all that he has made" (Ps 145:9). Implicit to this text is that God's saving purpose is extended to all humankind.

Philosophical Reflections on Predestination, Grace, and God's Universal Salvific Will

Four theological questions emerge from the biblical data exegeted in this chapter that Scripture itself does not answer. Hence we may turn again to philosophy to assist in answering these questions. The first question we shall analyze runs as follows: When Scripture speaks of predestination being based on foreknowledge (including knowledge of prior facts), what kind of foreknowledge is in view? Is this foreknowledge of hypothetical conditionals about creatures or foreknowledge of the future about creatures? Recall our assumption that predestination is God's choice to elect or reprobate each individual. If foreknowledge here refers to foreknowledge of the future about creatures, then God would know prior to his predestinary choice who will in the future embrace his salvation, reject his salvation, or not exist, which is self-refuting. For then there would be no choice for God to make with regard to both creation and predestination. If God already knows who will and will not exist prior to his decision to create a particular world of creatures, then there is no possibility for that decision. God would already be apprised of the world that will exist, and it will do so independently of God's choice. In that case, creation could not transpire. Likewise, if God already knows who, among existent creatures, will and will not receive salvation prior to his decision to elect or reprobate each creature, then there is no possibility for that decision. God would already be apprised of each person's salvific status, and they will reach that status independently of God's choice. In that case, predestination could not transpire.

But suppose that foreknowledge here refers to foreknowledge of hypothetical conditionals about creatures. Then God foreknows, for any possible set of circumstances, how each possible person would respond to God's salvific offer therein prior to God's decision to elect, reprobate, or not create that person. As we learn from Jesus, some of the same persons would respond differently to God's salvific offer in different circumstances:

> Then he began to reproach the cities in which most of his deeds of power had been done, because they did not repent. "Woe to you, Chorazin! Woe to you, Bethsaida! For if the deeds of power done in you had been done in Tyre and Sidon, they would have repented long ago in sackcloth and ashes. But I tell you, on the day of judgment it will be more tolerable for Tyre and Sidon than for you. And you, Capernaum, will you be exalted to heaven? No, you will be brought down to Hades. For if the deeds of power done in you had been done in Sodom, it would have remained until this day. But I tell you that on the day of judgment it will be more tolerable for the land of Sodom than for you." (Matt 11:20–24; see also Luke 10:13–15)

As I have written elsewhere, "Here Jesus articulated his knowledge that if he had performed his miracles in different spatio-temporal locations than in those where he actually performed them, then certain groups of individuals who had not in fact repented and were damned would have repented and been saved."[20] This observation is consistent with, but does not necessarily entail, the notion that for every possible person P, P would freely appropriate salvation in some circumstances, P would freely reject salvation in some circumstances, and P would not exist in some circumstances.[21] If this notion is true, it is then up to God's predestinary choice for every P whether P is elect, reprobate, or non-existent, which God carries out in the first and second instances by creating circumstances in which P's contingent choice is to respectively accept or reject God's salvation.[22] Hence foreknowledge

---

20. MacGregor, *Molina*, 83.

21. Proponents of the doctrine of transworld damnation deny this claim, holding that some P would freely reject salvation in every set of circumstances. See Craig, "No Other Name," 181–84. In chapter 6, I delineate a way, formulated by Aaron Fitzwater, that a literal interpretation of Matt 11:20–24 is compatible with transworld damnation.

22. MacGregor, *Molina*, 150, 156–57.

of hypothetical conditionals renders possible divine creation and individual predestination. From this it follows that the foreknowledge depicted in biblical discussions of individual predestination, assuming there are any such discussions, is foreknowledge of hypothetical conditionals.

We now turn to the second question: How can predestination be both in accordance with and not based upon foreknowledge of prior facts about the elect and the reprobate? At this juncture the philosophical notion of feasible worlds proves beneficial. God's knowledge of discrete facts about who would exist and what would happen in various circumstances naturally, given God's supremely logical mind, coalesces into knowledge of compossible, or logically consistent and so combinable, descriptions of how reality would be. To illustrate, the individual fact of my parents' meeting each other in various circumstances is compossible with the individual fact of my existing in consequent circumstances. But the individual fact of my parents' never meeting each other in different circumstances is not compossible with the individual fact of my existing in consequent circumstances. Each complete and logically consistent description of the way reality would be is known as a feasible world. In view of our answer to the first question, let us suppose that for any possible person P, P is freely saved in some feasible worlds, freely lost in some feasible worlds, and non-existent in some feasible worlds. Suppose further that God does not take into account his knowledge of these facts when choosing which feasible world to create. God in his sovereignty simply decides which world he prefers. Notice that God's individual predestination—his election and reprobation—is part and parcel of God's creative choice. For by deciding to create a particular world, God chooses to actualize circumstances in which every P is freely saved, freely lost, or non-existent. For any existing P, God could have just as easily chosen to create a different feasible world where P would freely come to have the opposite salvific status or not exist. Thus no elect P can say, "I saved myself by freely pledging allegiance to Christ," because (among other reasons)[23] God could have created a different feasible world where P could have been freely saved but is freely damned. So election in the final analysis "depends not on human will or exertion, but on God who shows mercy" (Rom 9:16).[24] From the foregoing inquiry it follows that election and reprobation are not based upon foreknowledge of hypothetical

---

23. The most important of which being prevenient grace and the life, death, and resurrection of Jesus, divine choices without which no one would be saved.

24. MacGregor, *Molina*, 148–51.

Molinist Philosophical and Theological Ventures

conditionals. However, election and reprobation agree with, and hence are in accordance with, foreknowledge of hypothetical conditionals.[25]

The third and fourth questions shall be considered together: How can electing some and reprobating others be consistent with God's universal salvific will? And how can electing some and reprobating others be not unjust, as Paul insisted? God's universal salvific will entails that God desires a world that attains to optimal salvation. Optimal salvation could be mathematically defined as containing the most saved (regardless of whether they are strong believers or believers barely escaping through the flames [1 Cor 3:15]) with the fewest lost. It could also be relationally defined as containing saved persons with the deepest, most passionate relationships with God. It could be a combination of these or something else resembling one of these. In any event, optimal salvation is not an empty concept—God knows exactly what it means. Now some people are saved only if various lost people exist. To illustrate, suppose that Bob's father is lost and Bob is saved in any world in which they both exist. Bob's existence logically presupposes the existence of his father, making it impossible for both Bob and his father to be saved. And this is only a simple example—obviously things get increasingly complex the more people one takes into consideration. So it is logically impossible (and thus beyond the scope of omnipotence) for God to simply pick out everyone who would be freely saved in any feasible world and ensure their salvation by putting them all together into the same world, since in that world many of those persons would be freely lost. God's attaining the free salvation of some entails God's permitting the free damnation of others.

Notice that God's reprobation of someone does not make that person be lost or explain why that person is lost. It is important to stress that God's reprobating an individual is not a direct divine action but is an indirect and unintended side-effect of God's electing others. As we saw in our discussion of grace, God gives prevenient grace, or grace necessary for salvation, to all persons indiscriminately. The reprobate may even be given a "greater measure of grace than given the elect. It is simply that

---

25. MacGregor, *Molina*, 152–53. I then go on to explain, "when Romans 9:11–13 says that 'before the twins were born or had done anything good or bad—in order that God's purpose in election might stand: not by works but by him who calls . . . Jacob I loved, but Esau I hated'" [NIV], it only affirms that election is *not based on* prior knowledge of their actions. It does not affirm that God *lacks prior knowledge* of their actions, and it seems that no one who affirms a traditional understanding of God's omniscience . . . could deny that God has prior knowledge of their actions" (153).

the reprobate freely choose to reject God as the Lord of their lives."[26] God wants each one of the reprobate in any feasible world to be saved but knows that this would not happen. Considering at least the pre-mortem life, God's desire for universal salvation winds up being thwarted. In that case, which feasible world, if any, is God going to pick? We know that God would only consider worlds reaching optimal salvation. All such worlds possess equal value. Because there is a potential infinity of such worlds, it is reasonable to suppose that among those worlds, for every possible P there is at least one world where P is freely saved, at least one world where P is freely lost, and at least one world where P does not exist. Then "God cannot be gainsaid for electing some people and reprobating others, since all feasible worlds available to him at this stage are equally good, and God's electing some and reprobating others is simply the logically unavoidable consequence of his choice to create a world at all. Therefore the only way God can avoid electing some and reprobating others is by choosing not to create any world."[27] So should God refrain from creating any world? The answer is no, as William Lane Craig points out: "The blessedness and happiness of those who would accept Him [God] should not be precluded by those who would freely reject Him. Those who would willingly reject God and forfeit salvation should not be allowed to have a sort of 'veto power' over which worlds God is free to create."[28] Accordingly, God is not unjust in electing some and reprobating others. Since God desires the salvation of the reprobate and works to bring it about, election and reprobation are consistent with God's universal salvific will.

Conclusion: The Molinist Structure as the Best Explanation of the Evidence

Central to the Molinist structure are the claims that God possesses middle knowledge and that humans possess libertarian free will. We have already

---

26. MacGregor, *Molina*, 155. As William Lane Craig observes: "The lost are not created as mere means to some end, say, the salvation of the elect. Rather as persons created in God's image the lost are ends in themselves and are loved and valued by God, who wills their salvation and strives to achieve it. But of their own free will some people reject God's loving initiatives and are lost. It remains God's will and desire that all mankind, including those who finally separate themselves from God forever, be saved and come to the knowledge of the truth" (*Hard Questions*, 159–60).

27. MacGregor, *Molina*, 149.

28. Craig, *Hard Questions*, 161.

Molinist Philosophical and Theological Ventures

seen that the second key claim is biblically certified by the data on human freedom and grace. Middle knowledge refers to God's knowledge of hypothetical conditionals dealing with the actions of libertarian free creatures logically prior to God's decision to create the world. (Philosophers denominate such conditionals "counterfactuals of creaturely freedom" or CCFs.[29]) By process of elimination (disjunctive syllogism), we observed that the foreknowledge that Scripture regards as logically prior to predestination is precisely this knowledge of hypothetical conditionals dealing with the actions of libertarian free creatures. Since predestination comprises one facet of creation, God must possess such knowledge logically prior to creation. (Recall that this knowledge includes knowledge of all feasible worlds.) Hence the first key claim is certified as well. With the two key Molinist claims established, the rest of the Molinist structure follows by straightforward logic.

To say that one thing is logically prior to another is to say that the first is a necessary condition, or prerequisite, for the second. Is there any part of divine omniscience logically prior to middle knowledge, or what free creatures would do in various circumstances? Indeed there is. A prerequisite for God to have such knowledge is to know what free creatures could do in various circumstances. It would make no sense for me to say to my wife (a Presbyterian pastor), "I know that if you were to go to Wichita, you would stop by the Presbytery office" and then say "But I have no idea whether, if you were to go to Wichita, you could stop by the Presbytery office"! Logically, my knowledge of what she would do presupposes my prior knowledge of what she could do. So God's knowledge of what *could* be, which Molinists call God's natural (or necessary) knowledge,[30] is logically prior to God's knowledge of what *would* be, namely middle knowledge. Just as discrete facts in God's middle knowledge coalesce into feasible worlds (complete and logically consistent descriptions of how reality *would* be), so discrete facts in God's natural knowledge coalesce into possible worlds (complete and logically consistent descriptions of how reality *could* be). Thus God knows the range of possible worlds logically prior to God's knowing the range of feasible worlds. Consequently, we have the first two

---

29. Despite the name, "counterfactuals" include all hypothetical conditionals, both those that in fact obtain in the real world and those that do not in fact obtain in the real world.

30. Natural knowledge also encompasses all necessary truths, such as the laws of logic and mathematical truths. This point is uncontroversial among adherents to divine omniscience.

logical moments in the Molinist structure: natural knowledge followed by middle knowledge.

Now is there any part of divine omniscience logically posterior to middle knowledge? Again, there must be. Since God's middle knowledge is logically prior to his free choice to create a feasible world, what logically must obtain once God makes that choice? God's knowledge of what *would* happen if he were to create a certain feasible world plus God's decision to create that world yields God's knowledge of what *will* happen in that feasible world, which is now the actual world (the world that God in fact created). Molinists call this knowledge of what will happen (i.e., foreknowledge of future events) God's free knowledge, since it logically depends on God's free choice of which feasible world to create. That knowledge of what *will* be presupposes logically prior knowledge of what *would* be is seen in this self-contradictory statement to my wife, "I know that when you go to Wichita today, you will stop by the Presbytery office, but I have no clue whether, if you were to go to Wichita today, you would stop by the Presbytery office." Clearly I can only have the "will" knowledge if I already possess the "would" knowledge.

An intriguing question is, When in the logical structure does God know what God would do in various circumstances (counterfactuals of divine freedom)? As will be defended in the next chapter, God knows counterfactuals of divine freedom in his free knowledge. But I raise this question now because a central difference between Calvinists and Molinists is the interpretation of texts indicating that God foreknows, for any possible person and set of circumstances, how the person would respond if s/he were in that set of circumstances. Denying libertarian human freedom, Calvinists read these texts as God's foreknowledge of how God would causally determine the person to respond in various circumstances. Hence the statements made by these texts are known to God in God's free knowledge. Affirming libertarian human freedom, Molinists read these texts as God's foreknowledge of how the person would freely respond in various circumstances, i.e., instances of middle knowledge. To illustrate, the Calvinist reading of Matthew 11:20–24 is that God knows if Jesus' miracles were done in Tyre, Sidon, and Sodom and God were to causally determine the inhabitants' response, God would causally determine the inhabitants to repent. The Molinist reading is that God knows if Jesus' miracles were done in Tyre, Sidon, and Sodom, the inhabitants would freely repent. Needless to say, Molinists regard their reading as the only one consistent with the biblical data on human freedom and grace. But it should be noted that, on Molinism, God does possess the knowledge that Calvinists think these texts indicate. The Molinist affirms that, as part of God's creative decision, God decides what he would have done in all circumstances that he does not actualize.

According to the Molinist, God chose to create a world where he does not causally determine people's salvific responses. Yet God simultaneously chose how he would have acted in each world where he did causally determine people's salvific responses. Thus God, in his free knowledge, knows that in a world where Jesus' miracles were performed in Tyre, Sidon, and Sodom and God causally determined salvific responses, God would have causally determined the inhabitants to repent. Ironically, then, the Calvinist holds that God possesses less knowledge than the Molinist. The Molinist maintains that God foreknows both how each possible person, if endowed with libertarian freedom, would respond in every conceivable set of circumstances and how God would determine that each possible person, if lacking libertarian freedom, would respond in every conceivable set of circumstances. The Calvinist maintains that God only foreknows the latter. But recall that the only restrictions on divine omnipotence and omniscience are logical restraints: God can only do and know things that are respectively logically possible to do and know. At this juncture the Molinist would retort that it is certainly logically possible for God to create humans possessing libertarian freedom following the events of Genesis 3 (i.e., humans who either retain libertarian freedom notwithstanding the actions of Adam and Eve or have it divinely restored by prevenient grace). Accordingly, it is logically possible for God to know how such persons would respond to his salvific offer in various circumstances, even if God chooses never to create such persons.[31] Consequently, the Molinist believes that on Calvinism, there are logically knowable truths that God does not know, such that the Calvinist subscribes to a conception of a less than omniscient God.

---

31. As Craig observes: "What is a sufficient condition for a proposition to be logically knowable? So far as I can see, the only condition is that the proposition is true. What more is needed?" ("Middle-Knowledge View," 138). It seems that propositions about how possible libertarian individuals would freely respond to God's salvific offer either possess the value "true" or "false," such that an omniscient God would know all such true propositions. If the Calvinist replies that the grounding objection shows that these propositions are truth-valueless, then the arguments against the grounding objection in the next chapter defeat the reply.

Summing up the findings of this chapter, God's mental life regarding omniscience and his choice to create may be heuristically mapped out as follows:

- *Moment 1—Natural knowledge.* God knows all necessary truths and all possibilities (everything that *could* be). These facts coalesce into knowledge of all possible worlds.

- *Moment 2—Middle knowledge.* God knows all hypothetical conditionals regarding creaturely action (everything that *would* be regarding creaturely action). These facts coalesce into knowledge of all feasible worlds.

- *Divine creative decision.* Out of the potentially infinite range of all salvifically optimal feasible worlds (in which God wills and gives sufficient grace for salvation to every person), God sovereignly chooses to create, without regard to his knowledge of how any particular individual would respond to his salvific offer, one of these worlds. This choice entails that any individual who would respond affirmatively in that world is elect, and any individual who would respond negatively in that world is reprobate. Moreover, God decides what God would have freely done in any set of circumstances that does not obtain in the world he has chosen.

- *Moment 3—Free knowledge.* God knows all truths about the actual world (past, present, and future, and hence everything that *will* be).

This is precisely the Molinist structure of God's mental life. Hence the data of Scripture, illuminated by genuine philosophy, logically leads to Molinism. As I pointed out in my intellectual biography of Molina, Molina formulated this structure by using a parallel approach: starting with the biblical data, employing philosophy as a God-given subordinate tool to answer questions arising from that data, and then logically drawing together the biblical and philosophical threads.[32]

---

32. MacGregor, *Molina*, 79–105.

— 3 —

An Intuitionist Defense of Divine Supercomprehension

THE SPANISH JESUIT PHILOSOPHICAL theologian Luis de Molina (1535–1600) is most famous for his doctrine of middle knowledge, or God's prevolitional knowledge of what all possible creatures endowed with libertarian freedom would do in any set of circumstances. Today the most prominent rebuttal to middle knowledge is the grounding objection, which holds that counterfactuals of creaturely freedom (CCFs) lack any ground of their truth, or truthmakers, and so possess no truth value. But there are various philosophical exits one can take off the proverbial highway toward the grounding objection, each of which, if true, defeats the objection. The first three of these exits are pointed out by William Lane Craig. Craig observes that the grounding objection presupposes a particular version of the correspondence theory of truth known as truthmaker theory.[1] Truthmaker theory holds "that in addition to truth-bearers, whether these be sentences, thoughts, propositions, or what have you, there must also be entities in virtue of which such sentences and/or propositions is true," i.e., "truthmakers."[2] But truthmaker theory is a minority view among contemporary metaphysicians. Most metaphysicians regard Alfred Tarski's T-schema, i.e.,

---

1. Craig, "Truth-Makers," 339.
2. Craig, "Truth-Makers," 339–40.

p is true iff *p*, as rendering truthmakers unnecessary for truth.[3] If these metaphysicians are correct, then the grounding objection cannot, so to speak, even get off the ground. So one may simply reject truthmaker theory to defeat the grounding objection, a move which represents the first exit. But suppose one finds truthmaker theory persuasive. Even among truthmaker theorists, most are not truthmaker maximalists, who hold that every truth requires a truthmaker to be true. Most truthmaker theorists assert that there are some truths which are true without a truthmaker. And there is every reason to think that hypothetical conditionals (including CCFs) belong to this class.[4] Hence the second exit off the highway is rejecting truthmaker maximalism, which the grounding objection presupposes. Yet suppose one embraces truthmaker maximalism. Then one may claim that the facts or states of affairs revealed by the disquotation principle constitute the grounds for CCFs. Thus the ground of the CCF "If I had a stuffed animal in my office and it was a cat, I would name it Guido" is the fact that if I had a stuffed animal in my office and it was a cat, I would name it Guido. Facts and states of affairs are considered by truthmaker theorists as perfectly legitimate truthmakers.[5] Identifying such grounds amounts to the third exit.

The remaining exits are inspired by Molina himself. To the question of how God can possess middle knowledge (an early form of the grounding objection), Molina responded with the so-called doctrine of divine supercomprehension, namely, "an *absolutely profound and absolutely preeminent comprehension*, such as is found only in God with respect to creatures."[6] This comprehension refers to "God's unlimited capacity to perceive infinitely, within his own mind, the individual essence . . . [of] every possible thing he could create."[7] As a divine conceptualist, Molina held that "these individual essences exist neither independently of God nor outside of God but only as designs within the mind of God."[8] Such individual essences are eternally generated by God's imagination—potentialities God knows he

---

3. Craig, "Truth-Makers," 343. For an outstanding critique of truthmaker theory, see Perrine, "Undermining Truthmaker Theory," 185–200.

4. Craig, "Truth-Makers," 344. For an outstanding critique of truthmaker maximalism, see Milne, "Not Every Truth," 221–24.

5. Craig, "Truth-Makers," 346, 340.

6. Molina, *Foreknowledge*, 171 (4.52.11).

7. MacGregor, *Molina*, 100.

8. MacGregor, *Molina*, 101.

Molinist Philosophical and Theological Ventures

could actualize if he so desired. We immediately find that, for Molina, God procures no knowledge from any creatures he might subsequently cause to emerge from these potentialities, but God procures knowledge solely from his awareness of the potentialities themselves located squarely in God's own self.[9] As Molina explained:

> God does not get His knowledge from things, but knows all things *in* Himself and *from* Himself; therefore, the existence of things, whether in time or eternity, contributes nothing to God's knowing with certainty what is going to be or not going to be. For prior to any existence on the part of the objects, God has within Himself the means whereby He knows all things fully and perfectly.... Through His natural [i.e., middle] knowledge *God comprehends Himself,* and *in Himself* He comprehends all the things that exist *eminently in Him* and thus the free choice of any creature whom He is able to make through His omnipotence. Therefore, before any free determination of His will, by virtue of the depth of His natural [i.e., middle] knowledge, by which He infinitely surpasses *each of the things He contains eminently in Himself,* He discerns what the free choice of any creature would do by its innate freedom, given the hypothesis that He should create it in this or that order of things with these or those circumstances or aids—even though the creature could, if it so willed, refrain from acting or do the opposite, and even though if it was going to do so, as it is able to freely, God would foresee *that* very act and *not* the one that He *in fact* foresees would be performed by that creature.[10]

Because God's intelligence infinitely transcends each possible creature, God possesses knowledge of CCFs. It should be noted that God's intelligence does not infinitely transcend God, such that God does not supercomprehend God's own self. Thus God does not have middle knowledge of God's own future decisions, a situation which Molina thought would destroy divine freedom.[11]

Most contemporary philosophers, following Robert Adams, regard supercomprehension as impossible on the grounds that it posits God as knowing about each possible creature things that are not objectively there to be known about those creatures, namely, CCFs.[12] By contrast, John Laing has

---

9. MacGregor, *Molina*, 101.
10. Molina, *Foreknowledge*, 119–20 (4.49.11-12).
11. Molina, *Foreknowledge*, 173–74 (4.52.13).
12. Adams, "Middle Knowledge," 111.

defended supercomprehension by arguing that each possible creature is an idea in the mind of God, an idea that "includes *in it* all the true counterfactuals regarding how the creature it represents would in fact act."[13] Accordingly, CCFs are objectively there to be known and ultimately grounded in the divine mind. Nonetheless, CCFs "retain their contingent status because although they are grounded in God, they receive their truth values from the creaturely wills which pre-exist in the divine mind as ideas."[14] Although Molina's fellow Spanish Jesuit philosophical theologian Francisco Suárez (1548–1617) parted company with Molina on the truth of supercomprehension, Laing's defense draws on Suárez's doctrine of habitudes,[15] or the unique properties of possible creatures whereby God knows their conditionally future free decisions.[16] As a divine conceptualist,[17] I concur with Laing that each possible creature is an idea—more specifically, an individual essence—in God's mind. I also find great promise in Laing's account of how CCFs are ultimately grounded in God. Thus Laing's account represents the fourth exit one may take off the highway to the grounding objection.

However, the objection could be raised that Laing "breaks the rules," so to speak, of what an individual essence can comprise by claiming that such an essence includes contingent, and therefore accidental, properties. For an essence, typically understood, includes only properties necessary to that essence's instantiation, without which the essence could not be instantiated. If the habitudes are in fact part of each individual essence, then it may be argued that the instantiation of each essence must act accordingly by logical necessity, which amounts to determinism.[18] It seems to me that this objection fails because the essence, or idea, itself determines the accidental properties (habitudes) rather than the habitudes determining

---

13. Laing, "Molinism and Supercomprehension," 338. This notion builds off Jonathan Kvanvig's argument that creaturely individual essences include all the CCFs regarding what their instantiations would do in any set of circumstances (*All-Knowing God*, 124–25).

14. Laing, "Molinism and Supercomprehension," 338.

15. Laing, "Molinism and Supercomprehension," 310–13.

16. Matava, *Divine Causality*, 145; see also Suárez, *Opera Omnia*, 7:94–96. For reasons we will uncover later, Suárez held to the doctrine of middle knowledge through comprehension rather than supercomprehension (Craig, *Divine Foreknowledge*, 269).

17. I concur with Stephen Parrish's recent argument that theistic conceptualism "is the best choice for the perfect being theist" ("Defending Theistic Conceptualism," 117).

18. As William Hasker objected to Kvanvig, "no individual chooses, or is responsible for, what is contained in that individual's essence" (*God, Time, and Knowledge*, 32).

the essence. So long as the causal arrow moves from the essence to the habitudes, I think the notion of an essence can be expanded to include such accidental properties. But what if one is persuaded by the objection? Then one could argue that each individual essence owns but does not include the CCFs appertaining to it, which constitutes a fifth exit.

Suppose the accidental character of the habitudes can be rescued. If so, they might fall prey to the charge of incoherence leveled by Adams, Linda Zagzebski, and Robert Joseph Matava, since the habitudes then seemingly cannot exist prior to God's decision to create.[19] Suppose *arguendo* that this charge and/or the previous objection is cogent.[20] How might one avert them? In this chapter I propose a way forward that, I believe, retains the strengths of Laing's defense of supercomprehension while eliminating its alleged weaknesses. This way forward is the sixth, but by no means final, exit off the highway to the grounding objection.[21] Employing perfect being theology, I shall argue that CCFs are grounded not in properties of individual essences but in God's infallible yet contingent beliefs about individual essences logically prior to God's creative decision. Such beliefs are timeless divine ideas that constitute the truthmakers of CCFs. Drawing on contemporary psychological and philosophical reflection, I contend that these beliefs are formed by God's intuition, a divine cognitive faculty that makes cogent judgments in evidentially underdeterminative cases. My case builds upon concepts first articulated by Suárez in defense of middle knowledge, thus employing Suárez (despite himself) in support of supercomprehension. I shall then respond to various objections to supercomprehension, including its prevention of God from possessing complete self-knowledge and its leading to determinism.

Perfect Being Theology and Divine Beliefs

Perfect being theology maintains in Anselmian fashion that God is, by definition, the greatest conceivable being who exemplifies every perfection. On perfect being theology, divine omniscience entails by logical necessity that God believes every truth and believes no falsehoods. However, William

---

19. Adams, "Middle Knowledge," 111–12; Zagzebski, *Dilemma of Freedom and Foreknowledge*, 143; Matava, *Divine Causality*, 146.

20. I believe that my proposed "fifth exit" answers this charge.

21. See Laing, *Middle Knowledge*, 65–102, for a survey of available Molinist responses to the grounding objection.

An Intuitionist Defense of Divine Supercomprehension

Alston would disagree with this entailment, denying that God has any beliefs. He contends that divine knowledge is exclusively comprised by God's immediate awareness of all facts, without any mental representation such as beliefs about them.[22] In support of this thesis, Alston presents arguments on two fronts, each of which has in my judgment correctly been criticized by Travis Dickinson.[23] First, Alston claims that his view follows from God's perfection. Unlike human knowledge, which cannot be exhausted by direct awareness because we are directly aware of very few facts, God's knowledge does not possess this limitation and so can be exhausted by divine awareness.[24] Such awareness does not permit even the potential for falsehood.[25] Second, Alston alleges that divine beliefs are needless:

> The point is that if God is immediately aware of all facts, there is no point in His *assenting* to propositions. Such activity has a point only when one does not already have effective access to the facts. If one's best shot at reality is to pick out those propositions that, so far as one can tell, have the best chance of being true and assenting to them, well and good. But if one already has the facts themselves, what is the point of *assenting* to propositions? It would be a meaningless charade.[26]

Regarding the first argument, Dickinson retorts that Alston has not proven enough to show his view, and not some other view which features both direct awareness and beliefs, is correct. About the latter view Dickinson comments, "This would be everything his [Alston's] view has and more still. The direct awareness with facts plus the corresponding propositional attitudes would seem, on its surface, to be a richer overall cognitive state for God."[27] However, I would add that Alston has failed to show that there may not be facts whose logical structure entails that they be apprehended through a belief-forming faculty. If there are such facts, then God's perfection does not guarantee that all facts are contained within God's immediate awareness. All God's perfection shows is that God knows such facts, not that God knows them immediately.[28] Further, Dickinson maintains that

---

22. Alston, "Does God Have Beliefs," 294–95.
23. Dickinson, "God Knows."
24. Alston, "Does God Have Beliefs," 297–98.
25. Alston, "Does God Have Beliefs," 296.
26. Alston, "Does God Have Beliefs," 298.
27. Dickinson, "God Knows," 4.
28. Although Dickinson would almost certainly disagree with me on this point, as

Alston achieves God's infallibility at too steep a price. Granted, on Alston's view God's knowledge cannot contain falsehood, but neither can it contain truth, since truth and falsehood are properties of beliefs and propositions. Dickinson explains: "A counterintuitive result of Alston's account is that God wouldn't know *all truths* (or any truths, for that matter), since there are no beliefs or propositional attitudes in view. God wouldn't be able to believe falsely, but this is because he has no beliefs to start with."[29] Thus divine knowledge of all truths is predicated on divine beliefs.

Dickinson summarizes the second argument as the superfluity thesis, according to which "if one is directly aware of a fact x, then a propositional attitude about x is unnecessary for knowing x."[30] But Dickinson insists that one may possess direct awareness of a fact and still fail to know this fact.[31] He furnishes the following instances of direct awareness sans knowledge:

> We are all immediately aware of facts right now about which we have not formed any thoughts, about which we haven't conceptualized. One should consider a patch of colour in the periphery of one's visual field (or the buzzing of lights or of an electrical device), which one has not (until just now) noticed, though it has been there all along as an object of awareness. Though we were (by hypothesis) directly aware of them, these non-conceptualized facts were not plausibly objects of knowledge since we didn't even notice them or form any thoughts about them. It seems that it is in the forming of thoughts that these become possible objects of knowledge. For another example, newborn babies are aware of many features of the world for which they possess no concepts. The baby, it seems, is only aware in the direct sense since he or she does not yet have the conceptual resources to form thoughts about these features. Though the baby is immediately aware of certain facts, the mere awareness is not plausibly knowledge of those facts.[32]

On Alston's view, God would seem to be in exactly the same boat, being "merely aware without any kind of propositional attitudes."[33] If "mere direct

---

implied by his claim that something "needs to be added to Alston's account to achieve the epistemic ideal" ("God Knows," 7), my proposal in this chapter meets Dickinson's three conditions for divine knowledge ("God Knows," 11).

29. Dickinson, "God Knows," 4.
30. Dickinson, "God Knows," 5.
31. Dickinson, "God Knows," 5.
32. Dickinson, "God Knows," 6.
33. Dickinson, "God Knows," 6.

awareness is not sufficient for knowledge" in the human cases, why is it plausible to suppose that it would be sufficient in God's case?[34] Unless we beg the question, it appears that belief is essential to knowledge for any knower.[35]

Open theism holds, among other things, that free future decisions are logically unknowable even to God. Some open theists maintain, on the basis of biblical passages like Isaiah 5:2–5; 63:8–10; Jeremiah 3:3–20; 7:31; 32:35; and Ezekiel 22:30–31, that God's beliefs are sometimes wrong.[36] It is far from obvious that these open theists' exegesis of such texts is correct.[37] But even if there is no other plausible way that these passages can be interpreted, this situation would only compromise biblical inerrancy, which constitutes no part of perfect being theology. Hence perfect being theology requires the premise that for any proposition p,

1. Necessarily, God believes p if and only if p is true.

Consider some creaturely individual essence including the property of libertarian freedom, which I shall denominate a creaturely libertarian essence (CLE). Given some fully specified set of circumstances C and some action A, let p assume either of the following two types, one positive (type P) and one negative (type N):

- Type P: If the instantiation of the CLE were in C, then the instantiation of the CLE would do A.
- Type N: If the instantiation of the CLE were in C, then the instantiation of the CLE would not do A.

Suppose that, logically prior to God's creative decision,

2. p is true.

From premises 1 and 2 it follows that

3. Therefore, God believes p.

---

34. Dickinson, "God Knows," 6.

35. Dickinson, "God Knows," 7.

36. Sanders, *God Who Risks*, 45–49, 132, 205; Basinger, "Practical Implications," 165. Other open theists maintain these texts show only that God believed various things would probably happen that did not in fact come to pass, and that such probabilistic beliefs were true (Boyd, "Christian Love," 237; Pinnock, *Most Moved Mover*, 50–52).

37. Erickson, *What Does God Know*, 17–38.

Molinist Philosophical and Theological Ventures

At this juncture it might be objected that God necessarily believes *p*, which, when combined with premise 1, yields the conclusion that *p* is necessarily true. Accordingly, type P and type N propositions could not be contingent and would be rendered self-contradictory, since they claim to describe contingent action or inaction (i.e., action or inaction by a CLE). But this objection commits a fallacy in modal logic. It conflates the necessity of the inference to God's believing *p* (the *necessitas consequentiae*) with the necessity of God's believing *p* (the *necessitas consequentis*), despite that the former does not entail the latter. Hence the contingency of type P and type N propositions remains unthreatened.

As Matava explains, Suárez maintained that "the law of excluded middle—that of a pair of contradictory propositions one must necessarily be true and the other false—requires that one member of each pair of opposed future conditionals be true."[38] However, it could now be objected that neither a type P nor a type N proposition need be true for the instantiation of some CLE and fully specified set of circumstances. Indeed, according to the standard Stalnaker-Lewis semantics for conditionals, the propositions $x \mathrel{\Box\!\!\rightarrow} y$ and $x \mathrel{\Box\!\!\rightarrow} {\sim}y$ (where $\mathrel{\Box\!\!\rightarrow}$ is read "If it were the case that (antecedent), then it would be the case that (consequent)") are not contradictories but contraries. Even though both propositions could be false, if either proposition is true the other is false. Proceeding along Suárezian lines, some philosophers have rejected this feature of the semantics and defended the principle of Conditional Excluded Middle (CEM), according to which $x \mathrel{\Box\!\!\rightarrow} y$ and $x \mathrel{\Box\!\!\rightarrow} {\sim}y$ are in fact contradictories.[39] In defense of the semantics, other philosophers have attempted to furnish counterexamples to CEM.[40] Suppose for the sake of argument that the counterexamples succeed. I deny that they succeed, for they are ambiguous and thus arguably not propositions.[41] But even if we reject CEM in these exceptional cases, it still remains the case that the principle works for any would-counterfactual whose structure is sufficiently clear to guarantee either its truth or the truth of its Stalnaker-Lewis contrary. I call such a counterfactual a "well-formed" counterfactual. Thomas Flint and Alfred Freddoso have argued, persuasively in my judgment, that type

---

38. Matava, *Divine Causality*, 149; see also Suárez, *Opera Omnia*, 11:357.

39. Gaskin, "Conditionals," 416–29; Kowalski, "Suarezian Middle Knowledge," 219–28; Cross, "Conditional Excluded Middle," 173–88; Laing, *Middle Knowledge*, 65–69.

40. Lewis, *Counterfactuals*, 80–82; Adams, "Middle Knowledge," 110; Hess, "Arguing," 334–51.

41. Craig, *Divine Foreknowledge*, 254; Laing, "Molinism and Supercomprehension," 167–242.

P and type N propositions (pairs of which are Stalnaker-Lewis contraries) meet precisely this criterion.[42] To their argument I would add that the circumstances in the antecedent of a type P or type N proposition include the entire history of the world up to the moment of an agent's choosing whether or not to undertake some action. As William Lane Craig points out, "For since the circumstances C in which the free agent is placed are fully specified in the counterfactual's antecedent, it seems that if the agent were placed in C and left free with respect to action A, then he must either do A or not do A. For what other alternative is there?"[43]

It follows from this that an omniscient God believes either a type P or type N proposition for every CLE, set of circumstances, and action prior to God's creative decision. Contra some open theists, it is not enough for God to withhold judgment and only believe—as God also does—that type P and type N propositions might and might not be true. For God knows that it is logically necessary that one of the two is true and the other false, though it is contingent which is which. Nevertheless, each CLE is evidentially underdeterminative, not supplying enough information in itself to determine which of the two is true. Even if the CLE rendered the intrinsic probability of its instantiation's doing A extremely high (though less than 1), the instantiation, as a libertarian agent, could always do otherwise.[44] So which of the two does God believe? To answer this question, we shall now turn to a discussion of intuition.

The Divine Intuition

Suárez first proposed that God knows future contingents "through a simple intuition of the truth or of the thing which will be at its proper time, as it will be at that time and according to all the conditions of existence which it will have at that time."[45] However, Suárez supplied no account of divine intuition, confessing ignorance regarding this mode of knowledge.[46] Among contemporary psychologists and philosophers, the definition of intuition is

---

42. Flint and Freddoso, "Maximal Power," 96.

43. Craig, "Truth-Makers," 338.

44. For this reason, Molina called what I refer to as a CLE "an object that *in its own right* is uncertain and deceptive" (*Foreknowledge*, 157 [4.51.18]).

45. Suárez, *Opera Omnia*, 11:327–28, translated by Craig, *Problem*, 212.

46. Craig, *Problem*, 212; Suárez, *Opera Omnia*, 11:328.

Molinist Philosophical and Theological Ventures

hotly contested.[47] Thus I use the term differently from Alston, Craig, and J. P. Moreland, who construe it as "a direct awareness of something that is directly present to consciousness."[48] Creatively adapting the insights of Daniel Kahneman, Ole Koksvik, Viktor Dörfler, Fran Ackermann, Jennifer Nagel, John Bengson, Michael Johnson, Jennifer Nado, Stephanie Tolan, and Miguel Egler, I propose that intuition is a cognitive faculty which generates judgments, or individual intuitions, in evidentially underdeterminative cases.[49] As Dörfler and Ackermann point out, intuition works instantaneously, spontaneously (meaning that it "does not require effort and cannot be deliberately controlled"), and alogically (meaning that it neither contradicts nor follows the rules of logic). The outcome of intuition "is *tacit* (in that the intuitives cannot give account of how they arrived at the results), *holistic* (also often called gestalt, as it is concerned with the totality of a situation rather than parts of it), and the intuitor feels *confident* about their intuition (with no apparent reason in terms of evidence)."[50] Tolan reports "that intuition very often . . . totally outperforms logic and reason."[51] A substance dualist, Tolan argues that intuition is a mental faculty that "cannot be explained by materialist science, and is part of our 'original equipment.'"[52] Though not always reliable, human intuition cannot fail to be generally reliable.[53] Since human souls, made in the *imago Dei*, possess a typically reliable yet sometimes fallible intuition, it stands to reason that God, as a perfect divine soul, must possess an infallible intuition.[54]

The phenomenology of individual intuitions is discussed by Egler in terms of four considerations accepted by virtually all contemporary

---

47. Booth and Rowbottom, *Intuitions*.

48. Moreland and Craig, *Philosophical Foundations*, 62; see also Alston, "Does God Have Beliefs," 294–95.

49. Kahneman, *Thinking*; Koksvik, "Intuition"; Bengson, "Experimental Attacks," 495–532; Dörfler and Ackermann, "Understanding Intuition," 545–64; Nagel, "Intuitions and Experiments," 495–527; Johnson and Nado, "Moderate Intuitionism," 68–90; Tolan, "Intuition," 25–42; Egler, "Testing for the Phenomenal," 48–66. I do not claim that any of these thinkers agree with my adaptation.

50. Dörfler and Ackermann, "Understanding Intuition," 547.

51. Tolan, "Intuition," 31.

52. Tolan, "Intuition," 39. She reports that many with high intuitive powers "consider these abilities to be explainable not by the human brain, but by the human spirit" (Tolan, "Intuition," 32).

53. Johnson and Nado, "Moderate Intuitionism," 68.

54. I concur with the model formulated by Moreland and Craig, *Philosophical Foundations*, 592–93, that God is a tripersonal divine soul.

phenomenalists. These considerations confirm and amplify Dörfler and Ackermann's analysis of the faculty of intuition. First, Egler deems intuitions to be "*conscious, non-perceptual propositional attitudes* that incline assent to what they represent. In other words, they are intentional states that do not involve any of the sensory modalities of perception, and that represent a proposition as true—thus motivating endorsement of that proposition."[55] Despite the fact that intuitions are non-perceptual, the cornerstone "of all recent phenomenalist accounts is the idea that intuitions and perceptual experiences are fundamentally similar kinds of mental states . . . *what it feels like* to have an intuition is similar to *what it feels like* to have a perceptual experience . . . both intuitions and perceptual experiences possess a (broadly defined) *presentational phenomenology*."[56] Second, Egler regards intuitions as "*spontaneous* in that we do not have to weigh considerations for or against a given proposition before having an intuition about it."[57] Third, Egler holds intuitions to be "*autonomous*, insofar as they are not responsive to contrary evidence."[58] Even if the intrinsic probability of something's occurrence is low, one may have an intuition that it would in fact happen. Fourth, Egler views intutions as "*seemingly truthful*, in that they purport to make subjects aware of facts."[59] According to Bengson, intuitions "tend to make formation of corresponding beliefs seem rational or fitting from the first-person perspective" and so "worthy of belief."[60] On the same score, Koksvik insists that any intuition "purports to represent an objective fact."[61] Contemporary phenomenalists, in Egler's words, concur "that intuitions are unlike mere guesses . . . which they contend are *not* seemingly truthful—as they at most incline one to believe or judge, without making their contents seem worthy of belief."[62]

Since evaluating CCFs—including type P and type N propositions—is to generate judgments in evidentially underdeterminative cases, I identify intuition with what Timothy Williamson calls "a general cognitive ability

---

55. Egler, "Testing for the Phenomenal," 51.

56. Egler, "Testing for the Phenomenal," 50.

57. Egler, "Testing for the Phenomenal," 51.

58. Egler, "Testing for the Phenomenal," 51.

59. Egler, "Testing for the Phenomenal," 51.

60. Bengson, "Intellectual Given," 723, as quoted in Egler, "Testing for the Phenomenal," 51.

61. Koksvik, "Intuition," 168, as quoted in Egler, "Testing for the Phenomenal," 51.

62. Egler, "Testing for the Phenomenal," 52.

to handle counterfactual conditionals."⁶³ Williamson explains this ability as follows: "When we have some conception of the circumstances in which r is true, and some conception of the circumstances in which s is true, we also have some conception of the circumstances in which the counterfactual $r \mathrel{\Box\!\!\rightarrow} s$ is true."⁶⁴ The verdicts generated by this ability "do not seem to be based on reasoning in any useful sense. Perhaps our ability to assess the truth-values of counterfactuals involves some capacity to simulate mentally the truth of the antecedent and to determine the truth-value of the consequent under that simulation."⁶⁵ E. J. Lowe characterizes this ability as one "that we deploy ubiquitously in everyday life."⁶⁶ Referring to what I have called a CLE as a "system," Kahneman furnishes a list of essential attributes of "System 1." He invites his readers to use their intuition to discern the truth of CCFs about System 1 (or more precisely, its instantiation): "My hope is that the list of traits will help you develop an intuitive sense of the 'personality' of the fictitious System 1. As happens with other characters you know, you will have hunches about what System 1 would do under different circumstances, and most of your hunches will be correct."⁶⁷ Quite suggestive for my proposal is Nagel's linking of intuition with mind reading and Tolan's association of intuition with psychic ability.⁶⁸ Note that I am not here endorsing the reality of psychic ability. The heart of both mind reading and psychic ability, if sometimes veridical, is the assessment of CCFs. Egler reports "the considerable amount of evidence that capacities for mind reading are very reliable—as shown by the accuracy of people's predictions of others' mental states."⁶⁹ Based on reports of children displaying seemingly psychic powers at the Hollingworth Conferences on the Highly Gifted and testimonies of professionals formerly known as psychics but now self-designating as intuitives, Tolan controversially suggests that psychic ability just is the fruit of an extremely refined intuition.⁷⁰ Regardless of one's view of psychic ability, this suggestion shows the potential lengths to which some theorists extend the power of intuition.

63. Williamson, "Armchair Philosophy," 13.
64. Williamson, "Armchair Philosophy," 13.
65. Williamson, "Armchair Philosophy," 13.
66. Lowe, "Source of Knowledge," 919.
67. Kahneman, *Thinking*, 105.
68. Nagel, "Intuitions and Experiments," 510–11; Tolan, "Intuition," 30.
69. Egler, "Testing for the Phenomenal," 61.
70. Tolan, "Intuition," 29–30.

An Intuitionist Defense of Divine Supercomprehension

Dörfler and Ackermann insist that intuition is a faculty that often yields knowledge.[71] Tolan agrees: "What intuition can bring is often a level of accuracy that no amount of rational thought could glean from a particular situation. And there seems to be *no way to explain* this knowing that arrives seemingly out of nowhere."[72] Indeed humans, with far inferior intellects to God, can apprehend the essences of other humans well enough to use intuition in seemingly gaining a finite amount of counterfactual knowledge about them. For instance, I apprehend my wife's essence well enough to intuit that if I were to offer my wife a glass of Dr Pepper and a glass of Pepsi, she would choose the glass of Dr Pepper—a proposition which is underdetermined by my wife's essence.[73] Indeed, it seems to me that I know this proposition with as much certainty as anything I know! So if we human beings, with our finite intelligence and finite apprehension of other human essences (which were not generated by our imagination), can intuit what their instantiations would freely do in some sets of circumstances, it seems eminently reasonable to maintain that God, with God's infinite intelligence and complete knowledge of all human essences (which are eternally generated by God's imagination), can intuit what their instantiations would freely do in any set of circumstances in which they find themselves.[74]

At this point it may be objected that God's beliefs acquired by intuition do not constitute knowledge and so cannot serve as the basis for middle knowledge. Now knowledge is typically regarded by epistemologists as either warranted true belief or some version of justified true belief that evades the so-called Gettier counterexamples.[75] It follows from premise 1 of our earlier syllogism that God's believing any proposition entails that proposition's truth. Hence all God's intuited beliefs are true, and God's intuited beliefs about type P and type N propositions constitute the truthmakers of CCFs. Alvin Plantinga maintains that a belief has warrant if the belief is produced by one or more cognitive faculties that are properly functioning and are functioning in circumstances in which those faculties are suited to operate.[76] As a perfect being, all of God's cognitive faculties,

---

71. Dörfler and Ackermann, "Understanding Intuition," 547.

72. Tolan, "Intuition," 39.

73. MacGregor, *Molina*, 103.

74. MacGregor, *Systematic Theology*, 75–76.

75. Plantinga, *Warranted Christian Belief*, xi; Turri, "Is Knowledge Justified True Belief?," 247–59.

76. Plantinga, *Warranted Christian Belief*, xi.

including God's intuition, must function perfectly. Since intuition is suited to operate on evidentially underdeterminative cases, God's intuition regarding CLEs are functioning in appropriate circumstances. Accordingly, God's intuited beliefs are warranted and so, on the first definition of the term, constitute knowledge. Regarding the second definition of knowledge, I concur with Craig that God possessed justification for God's true beliefs because, among God's store of beliefs, is premise 1 of our earlier syllogism. Since God knows God's own identity simply by acquaintance, God is justified on the basis of premise 1 in holding the beliefs that God does.[77] This case is not affected by the Gettier problems. Consequently, God's intuited beliefs constitute knowledge on the second definition. On either the first or second definition, then, God's intuited beliefs adequately ground God's middle knowledge.

Limitation of God's Self-Knowledge?

We now confront challenges to supercomprehension heretofore unaddressed. The first was raised by Suárez: does God's supercomprehension of what I have called CLEs issue in a more complete knowledge of them than God has of God's own self?[78] I believe Laing has effectively answered this question in the negative. As Laing points out, Molina subscribed to the belief that divine eternality denotes timelessness, such that the moments of God's knowledge are logical rather than temporal.[79] It is indeed true that at the moment of omniscience logically prior to God's creative decision (i.e., middle knowledge), God has not apprehended futurefactuals or counterfactuals of divine freedom. But at the moment of omniscience logically posterior to God's creative decision (i.e., free knowledge), God apprehends both of these.[80] For as part of God's creative decision, God decided what God will do (e.g., create a particular world) as well as what God would do in any conceivable set of circumstances. As Molina explained:

> For that free act regarding the things that are able to be done by God—an act in itself infinite, unlimited, and lacking any shadow of alteration—freely determined itself to one part of a contradiction with respect to all possible objects at once, not only (i) by

77. Craig, *Divine Foreknowledge*, 230.
78. Suárez, *Opera Omnia*, 11:372–74.
79. Laing, "Molinism and Supercomprehension," 292, 298–99.
80. Laing, "Molinism and Supercomprehension," 299.

freely establishing those things that He decided to bring about or to permit and by freely deciding not to bring out or permit the rest, but also (ii) by freely deciding which things He *would have* willed on any hypothesis that *could have* obtained and did not obtain. Indeed, the act in question reflects an absolutely complete and unlimited deliberation, made on the basis of both the purely *natural* knowledge and also that knowledge, in the *middle* between free knowledge and purely natural knowledge, which existed in God's intellect before (in our way of conceiving it, with a basis in reality) the act of His will.... Therefore, through His free knowledge, which follows upon the act of His will, He knows in that free determination of His will what He would have willed in any circumstances and under any hypothesis that could have obtained and did not obtain.[81]

Since, for Molina, God timelessly possesses middle knowledge and free knowledge, God's knowledge of CLEs was never greater than God's knowledge of God's own self.[82]

Does Supercomprehension Lead to Determinism?

On the contemporary scene, open theists charge on two fronts that middle knowledge, which I have rooted in supercomprehension, results in determinism. The first problem, *mutatis mutandis*, can be expressed in the following question: if supercomprehension of God's future decisions destroys God's freedom, then doesn't supercomprehension of future creaturely decisions destroy creaturely freedom?[83] The force of the question depends on the assumption that Molina's reason why supercomprehension of God's future decisions destroys God's freedom lies in the contradiction between a true proposition about a future action and that action's being done freely. However, Molina denied that there is any such contradiction.[84] Rather, Molina held that the reason supercomprehension of God's future actions destroys God's freedom is the principle that if a conscious being possesses prevolitional knowledge of that being's *own* future decisions, then those decisions are not made freely. In Laing's words, "The purpose of middle knowledge is to inform God's creative decision, but it does not make sense

81. Molina, *Foreknowledge*, 173–74 (4.52.13).
82. Laing, "Molinism and Supercomprehension," 299–300.
83. Boyd, "Neo-Molinism," 191.
84. Laing, "Molinism and Supercomprehension," 304.

to inform a decision with information about what that decision will be! That is, it is incoherent to expect God to know His will before He knows His will."[85] Hence God cannot supercomprehend God's own self because God's knowledge of God's own will cannot be prevolitional. Accordingly, we now see what Molina meant when he said that God's intelligence does not infinitely transcend God: God's intelligence does not intrude on or override God's libertarian freedom.

However, a conscious being's prevolitional knowledge of any other agent's future decisions does nothing to negate the freedom with which those decisions are made. For such knowledge is not causally determinative. Thus God's knowledge of what a person would do in some set of circumstances exerts no causal power on the person to act as God knows, just as human knowledge of what other humans would do exerts no causal power over their choices. My ostensible knowledge that my wife would choose Dr Pepper over Pepsi if I were to offer her those alternatives obviously does nothing to compel her to choose Dr Pepper if I elect to actualize the scenario. She chooses Dr Pepper just as freely as if I had no prior knowledge of the relevant CCF.[86] Likewise, Molina insisted that God's prior knowledge "imposes *no necessity or certitude of the consequent* on future things, but rather leaves them as uncertain in themselves and in relation to their causes as they would be if there were no such foreknowledge."[87]

The second problem is rooted in the fixed past principle, according to which the past is unpreventable or unchangeable since it is now too late to do anything about it.[88] Accordingly, if God believed type P and type N propositions logically prior to God's creative decision, then no creature has the power to change God's past beliefs, which are the truthmakers for CCFs. But this raises the question: what kind of "making" does truthmaker theory entail? As David Armstrong and John Bigelow emphasize, a proposition's truthmaker is that in virtue of which the proposition is true; it is not that which causes the proposition to be true.[89] The *in virtue of which* locution could be taken as either an ontological or a logical relation.

---

85. Laing, "Molinism and Supercomprehension," 305.

86. MacGregor, *Molina*, 103–4.

87. Molina, *Foreknowledge*, 193 (4.52.36).

88. Rice, *Openness*, 17; Hasker, *God, Time, and Knowledge*, 126; Boyd, "Open-Theism Response," 145–46.

89. Armstrong, *Truth and Truthmakers*, 5; Bigelow, *Reality*, 125.

An Intuitionist Defense of Divine Supercomprehension

Ontologically, God's belief constituting the truthmaker of a CCF means that the CCF's basis or foundation in reality is God's belief. Analogously, on the divine conceptualist's analysis, God's ideas constituting the truthmakers of the Peano axioms of arithmetic means that the axioms' bases or foundations in reality are God's ideas. Logically, God's belief constituting the truthmaker of a CCF means that the CCF corresponds to the relevant belief in God's mind. As Greg Welty points out, conceptualism holds that divine beliefs are abstract objects.[90] By definition, abstract objects are casually effete, such that God's beliefs do not cause CCFs to be true any more than God's ideas cause the Peano axioms to be true.

Moreover, neither the ontological nor the logical relation of truthmaking, I maintain, undermine a libertarian free creature's ability to exert counterfactual power over the past. For one need not be able to change the past in order to exert counterfactual power over it. Even though Molinism denies the possibility of backward causation (making the past no longer the past), it does furnish what I have called a "functional equivalent to backward causation."[91] Accordingly, it lies within the power of every libertarian free creature to freely perform some action A such that if A occurred, God's intuited belief about what that creature would do logically prior to God's creative decision would have been different than it in fact was.[92] To illustrate, suppose that God has always believed that in the year 2023 I would accept an invitation to speak at a theological institute. When I receive the call from the director offering me the invitation, I possess the ability to accept or reject the invitation. If I reject the invitation, then the past would have included God's intuited belief of my rejecting rather than accepting the invitation. As I have elsewhere written, "Without resorting to the incoherence of changing what the past *was* . . . via backward causation, the acausal character of the Molinist relation between creaturely choices and their corresponding counterfactual propositions entails that humans can perform the precisely comparable task of changing what the past would have been by way of their free decisions."[93] In short, truthmaking is not truth-causing, such that supercomprehension does not entail determinism.

---

90. Welty, "Theistic Conceptual Realism," 81.
91. MacGregor, *Systematic Theology*, 89.
92. MacGregor, *Systematic Theology*, 89–90.
93. MacGregor, *Systematic Theology*, 90.

Conclusion

This chapter has defended Molina's doctrine of divine supercomprehension by integrating the tools of perfect being theology with psychological and philosophical insights on intuition. Perfect being theology guarantees that an omniscient God believes either a type P or type N proposition for each CLE, set of circumstances, and action logically prior to God's creative decision, despite that this proposition is not included in the CLE. To figure out which one to believe, God employs intuition, a cognitive faculty which generates judgments in evidentially underdeterminative cases. It has been shown that God's intuited beliefs constitute knowledge, as they are true and are both warranted and justified. God's intuited beliefs stand as the truthmakers for CCFs, such that CCFs are ultimately grounded in God. Notwithstanding objections to the contrary, I have demonstrated that this scenario does not issue in determinism. Accordingly, the grounding objection is plausibly answered on its own terms. My solution—unwittingly inspired by Suárez—resonates with the historic Christian belief "that all truth is God's truth."[94]

---

94. Laing, "Molinism and Supercomprehension," 338.

— 4 —

Critiquing Explanatory Priority Arguments against Molinism

In the 1990s Robert Adams developed, and William Hasker enhanced, an argument against Molinism based on the concept of explanatory priority. Adams and Hasker—wrongfully in my judgment—held that explanatory priority is the type of priority Molinism presupposes in its sequence of natural knowledge, middle knowledge, the divine creative decision, and free knowledge, thus rendering explanatory priority fair game with which to attack Molinism. The salient premises of Adams' argument run as follows:

1. According to Molinism, the truth of all true counterfactuals of freedom about us is explanatorily prior to God's decision to create us.
2. God's decision to create us is explanatorily prior to our existence.
3. Our existence is explanatorily prior to all of our choices and actions.
4. The relation of explanatory priority is transitive.
5. Therefore, it follows from Molinism (by 1–4) that the truth of all true counterfactuals of freedom about us is explanatorily prior to all of our choices and actions.
10. It follows also from Molinism that if I freely do action A in circumstances C, then there is a true counterfactual of freedom F*, which says that if I were in C, then I would (freely) do A.

11. Therefore, it follows from Molinism that if I freely do A in C, the truth of F* is explanatorily prior to my choosing and acting as I do in C.

12. If I freely do A in C, no truth that is strictly inconsistent with my refraining from A in C is explanatorily prior to my choosing and acting as I do in C.

13. The truth of F* (which says that if I were in C, then I would do A) is strictly inconsistent with my refraining from A in C.

14. If Molinism is true, then if I freely do A in C, F* both is (by 11) and is not (by 12–13) explanatorily prior to my choosing and acting as I do in C.

15. Therefore, (by 14) if Molinism is true, then I do not freely do A in C.[1]

While Adams provided no definition of explanatory priority, Hasker supplied this definition: "p is explanatorily prior to q iff p must be included in a complete explanation of why q obtains."[2]

William Lane Craig and Thomas Flint both responded to this argument. Craig noted that premise 1 is false, as God may well have chosen to create us even if some or all true counterfactuals about us were false or even if no counterfactuals about us were true.[3] Thus the truth of all true counterfactuals about us or even there being true counterfactuals about us need not be included in a complete explanation of God's decision to create us. Craig argued that premise 4 is also false via *reductio ad absurdum*. Suppose the relation of explanatory priority is transitive. Craig wrote: "My wife and I not infrequently find ourselves in the situation that I want to do something if she wants to do it, and she wants to do it if I want to do it. Suppose, then, that John is going to the party because Mary is going, and Mary is going to the party because John is going. It follows that . . . John is going to the party because John is going to the party, which conclusion is obviously wrong."[4] Therefore, the relation of explanatory priority cannot be transitive. Hasker responded by contending that one of the two wished to go to the party first (e.g., several days before the party), thus leading the other to wish to go.[5] However, Hasker's response misses the point. Whoever wished to go to the

---

1. Adams, "Anti-Molinist Argument," 343–53.
2. Hasker, "Explanatory Priority," 3.
3. Craig, "Adams's New Anti-Molinist Argument," 859.
4. Craig, "Hasker's Defense," 238.
5. Hasker, "Anti-Molinism Undefeated," 128.

party first, it remains the case that, on the day of the party, Mary's going to the party must be included in a complete explanation of why John goes to the party, and John's going to the party must be included in a complete explanation of why Mary goes to the party. Moreover, the absurdity of John's going to the party being explanatorily prior to John's going to the party coupled with premise 12 leads to the conclusion "that John does not freely go to the party."[6] Given that Hasker's attempted definition of explanatory priority is unsuccessful, Flint proposes several other possible definitions and shows that, for each one, explanatory priority turns out to be neither transitive (thus refuting premise 4) nor capable of rendering all of premises 1 through 3 true. The only way all of premises 1 through 3 can be true is by using one sense of explanatory priority in premise 1 and a different sense in premises 2 and 3.[7] Unless and until a definition of explanatory priority can be offered which is both univocal and transitive, Craig and Flint concur that the reasoning of Adams and Hasker fails.[8]

Recently Philip Swenson, Andrew Law, Nevin Climenhaga, and Daniel Rubio have supplied two definitions which they believe meets the standard of univocality and transitivity.[9] Swenson, Climenhaga, and Rubio proceed from their respective definitions to present refurbished versions of the Adams-Hasker argument.[10] This chapter contends that the two new definitions are either equivocal or intransitive and that the refurbished Adams-Hasker arguments fail.

Swenson and Law: Explanatory Dependence and the Fixity of the Independent

Swenson and Law understand the explanatory priority of X to Y as the explanatory dependence of Y upon X. Law defines explanatory dependence as follows: "Roughly, a fact, F_1, is explanatorily *dependent* on another fact, F_2, just in case F_2 at least partly explains F_1; F_1 is thus explanatorily

---

6. Craig, "Hasker's Defense," 238.

7. Flint, *Divine Providence*, 164–71.

8. Craig, "Hasker's Defense," 239; Flint, *Divine Providence*, 171. Even if such a definition were found, Craig remarked that it would prove "so weak that it would not be inimical to human freedom" ("Hasker's Defense," 239).

9. Swenson, "Ability," 660–61; Law, "Fixity," 1302–3; Climenhaga and Rubio, "Molinism," 460–61.

10. Swenson, "Dilemma," 8:09—31:58; Climenhaga and Rubio, "Molinism," 466–82.

Molinist Philosophical and Theological Ventures

independent of F_2 just in case F_2 does not even partly explain F_1."[11] Listing logical, conceptual, metaphysical, and natural dependence, Swenson states that explanatory dependence is "the broad or generic notion that captures what all of these different cases of dependence (and perhaps other types of cases) have in common."[12] But now the question arises: do these cases have anything in common? As an example of logical dependence, Swenson gives "Sam is ill or 2 + 2 = 5 because Sam is ill."[13] Notice that "Sam is ill" is a necessary and sufficient condition for "Sam is ill or 2 + 2 = 5."[14] This example is somewhat misleading because logical dependence need only be a necessary condition. To illustrate, if God has middle knowledge, this is logically dependent on God's having natural knowledge. God can only know what *would* be if God already (logically speaking) knew what *could* be. Yet God's knowing what *could* be is not sufficient for God's knowing what *would* be.

While the mark of logical dependence is necessity, the mark of conceptual dependence is sufficiency. As an example of conceptual dependence, Swenson provides "The vase is coloured because it is red."[15] Notice that "The vase is red" is a sufficient but not necessary condition for "The vase is colored." Here we immediately see the incompatibility of logical and conceptual dependence—they simply have nothing in common. For "The vase is colored" is a necessary condition for "The vase is red," making the vase's being red logically dependent on the vase's being colored. Imagine for the sake of contradiction that there were a univocal notion of explanatory dependence emerging from logical and conceptual dependence. Then the vase's being red is explanatorily dependent on the vase's being colored (via logical dependence), and the vase's being colored is explanatorily dependent on the vase's being red (via conceptual dependence). However, any legitimate relation of explanatory dependence cannot be symmetric. Therefore,

---

11. Law, "Fixity," 1302.

12. Swenson, "Ability," 660. Law, "Fixity," 1302, adds "nomic/causal explanation" to the list.

13. Swenson, "Ability," 660.

14. Likewise, Swenson seems to understand metaphysical and natural dependence in terms of necessary and sufficient conditions. As an example of metaphysical dependence, Swenson gives "The set {Socrates} exists because Socrates does" ("Ability," 660). Socrates' existence is a necessary and sufficient condition for the set {Socrates} to exist. As an example of natural dependence, Swenson provides "Sam died because John stabbed him in the heart" ("Ability," 660). Assuming nothing bizarre (like Mary chopping off Sam's head simultaneously with John's stabbing Sam in the heart), John's stabbing Sam in the heart is a necessary and sufficient condition for Sam's death.

15. Swenson, "Ability," 660.

Critiquing Explanatory Priority Arguments against Molinism

the intersection of logical and conceptual dependence is the empty set. By the nature of the case, adding metaphysical and natural dependence to the mix does not help matters any. We must conclude that explanatory dependence, as defined by Swenson and Law, is equivocal and is thus an incoherent concept. Moreover, this notion of explanatory dependence cannot be transitive. For if it were, then the vase's being red would be explanatorily dependent on the vase's being red, which is absurd.

In 2016 Swenson proposed the principle of the Fixity of the Independent Past, which Law in 2021 generalized as the principle of the Fixity of the Independent.[16] The Fixity of the Independent holds, as Swenson states, that "an agent cannot (at time t) do anything incompatible with facts that are not even partially explained by A's choice at time t."[17] The veracity of this principle depends on what the phrase "even partially explained by" means. If "even partially explained by" ≡ "explanatorily dependent on," then the principle is incoherent by virtue of the equivocal nature of Swenson's version of explanatory dependence. So let us assume, for charity's sake, that something different from explanatory dependence is in view here and that the principle is coherent. Is it true or false? To find out, we must inquire whether any form of counterfactual dependence counts as even partially explanatory. Swenson rejects the explanatory nature of a version of counterfactual dependence according to which causal determinism holds, A performs some action X, and the proposition "If A had not performed X, the past would have been different than it in fact was" (i.e., the past would not have included the relevant causally determining conditions) is true.[18] Swenson rejects this version in order to ward off compatibilism. I agree that this version of counterfactual dependence is not legitimately explanatory. The reason is because A lacked the power to not perform X; such was barred by causal determinism.

So now the question arises: would Swenson accept or reject the explanatory nature of a different version of counterfactual dependence, which I shall dub genuine counterfactual dependence? According to genuine counterfactual dependence, causal determinism is false, it lies within A's power to do X or not do X, A does X, and if A had not done X, then the counterfactual of creaturely freedom (CCF) about what A would do would

---

16. Swenson, "Ability," 662; Law, "Fixity," 1302–3.

17. Swenson, "Dilemma," 8:28–38. Law, "Fixity," 1302, expresses this principle using possible world semantics.

18. Swenson, "Ability," 660.

have been different than it in fact was. Although he does not explicitly say, I strongly suspect that Swenson would reject the explanatory nature of genuine counterfactual dependence.[19] But in that case, the principle of the Fixity of the Independent is false. For then CCFs about A would not be even partially explained by A's choice at t, and yet A, possessing libertarian freedom, is in no way constrained by the CCFs. Facts are abstract objects and therefore causally effete. Facts about what A would do in a situation clearly have no magical power over A to make A do accordingly in that situation. Hence A could do something incompatible with the CCFs. So now let us suppose that Swenson would accept the explanatory nature of genuine counterfactual dependence. Then the Fixity of the Independent would be trivially true, asserting that A cannot at t do anything incompatible with facts over which A has neither causal nor counterfactual power. That much is already conceded by Molinists and non-Molinists alike.

As Alvin Plantinga points out, there are many things over which we cannot confidently assert that we have neither causal nor counterfactual power.[20] One might say we have little confidence over which facts are hard and which facts are soft. Swenson gives as examples of facts over which we currently have no power Reagan being President of the United States and the sun rising tomorrow. He uses these as test cases for the Fixity of the Independent, insisting that these facts are not even partially explained by our current choices and, consequently, that we cannot now do anything incompatible with them. But this does not strike me as obvious. Concerning Reagan, suppose that an elementary school girl now, having no knowledge of who won the 1980 US presidential election, learned in school about the run-up to that election. She has the ability to pray, "God, please have let Carter win the 1980 election and have never let Reagan be President." Suppose if she were to pray that, then God would have chosen a different feasible world in which Carter would have won re-election in 1980 and someone besides Reagan would have won the presidential election in 1984. If so, then the girl now has indirect counterfactual power over Reagan's being President.[21] All we can infer from Reagan's presidency is that the girl is

---

19. Swenson, "Ability," 660, 667.
20. Plantinga, "Ockham's Way Out," 268.
21. To give another illustration, suppose I am sitting at home waiting for my wife and son to return from the store. Five minutes ago I heard the sound of cars crashing, and now I hear the sound of the ambulance. I pray, "God, please let that accident not have included my wife and son." (I have prayed this on several occasions.) Suppose God, knowing that I would pray in this way, chooses to actualize a feasible world in which my

not now praying as I have suggested or that God would not have responded affirmatively to that prayer.[22] Concerning the sun rising tomorrow, suppose that I now pray, "Jesus, please return to earth tonight, bringing about the Second Coming." Suppose that the preincarnate Christ, knowing that I would pray this, decided to create a feasible world where the Second Coming happens tonight and the sun does not rise tomorrow. Suppose that, had I not prayed, the preincarnate Christ would choose a world in which the sun rises tomorrow and the Second Coming occurs far into the future. In that case, I have indirect counterfactual power over the sun's rising tomorrow. If the sun rises tomorrow, we can infer that I am not praying as I suggested or that Jesus would not have responded affirmatively to that prayer. As a result, the Fixity of the Independent only assures us that we lack power over indisputably hard facts, such as God's existence and other logically necessary truths. Since this is not a disputed point, the principle appears to possess no utility.

From a Molinist perspective, then, the Fixity of the Independent is either incoherent, false, or trivially true. In any case, it poses no threat to Molinism.

Swenson's First Argument against Molinism: A Dilemma

At this juncture Swenson poses a dilemma: "Are the CCFs involving our actual choices explained by our choices or not?"[23] To illustrate, Swenson imagines that he "actually tell[s] a lie in circumstance C" and that God knew L, namely, that he "would freely lie in C."[24] Then the question becomes: "is L explained by my choice to lie?"[25] On the one hand, suppose we answer

---

wife and son are not in that accident. However, suppose that if I had not prayed in this way, then God would have chosen a feasible world where my wife and son were in that accident. If so, I have indirect counterfactual power over my wife and son being in the accident.

22. Flint, *Divine Providence*, 229–50, effectively argues that, on Molinism, we can successfully pray for things to have occurred. Hasker ("New Anti-Molinist Argument," 294–95) rejoins that anything which has already exerted causal impact on the past (e.g., Reagan's presidency) is a hard fact over which we have no power. To this, Flint responds by persuasively arguing that "if God has middle knowledge, there are facts about the past which have had causal consequences in the past, but over which we do indeed have . . . counterfactual control" ("New Anti-Anti-Molinist Argument," 303).

23. Swenson, "Dilemma," 11:06–18.

24. Swenson, "Dilemma," 11:37–54.

25. Swenson, "Dilemma," 11:55–58.

in the negative, thereby presupposing that the "even partially explained by" clause of the Fixity of the Independent does not include genuine counterfactual dependence. Swenson argues that "If I can do anything other than lie, then I can do something incompatible with the truth of L."[26] Then he reasons from the Fixity of the Independent that "I cannot do anything incompatible with the truth of L."[27] He concludes, "Therefore, I cannot do anything other than lie."[28] However, under our presupposition the Fixity of the Independent is false, and with it Swenson's second premise. For even if L is not explained by Swenson's choice to lie, Swenson could still tell the truth. If Swenson were to tell the truth, then L would not have been a fact.

Readers familiar with arguments for fatalism will rightfully find similarities between those arguments and the first horn of Swenson's dilemma. For if L is a prior fact—regardless of God's existence—then, on an A-Theory of time (i.e., presentism), the Fixity of the Independent implies that a free agent is somehow constrained by it and cannot do otherwise. That is true regardless of whether L is a counterfactual (stating that Swenson would freely lie in C) or a futurefactual (stating that Swenson will freely lie in C).[29] Libertarian A-Theorists find the idea of L's constraining a free agent unintelligible. However, Swenson, himself a libertarian, escapes from the first horn of his dilemma by adopting a B-Theory of time (i.e., eternalism) and denying the existence of CCFs.[30] On the B-Theory, futurefactuals about our free choices exist and can be causally explained by our choices, as the temporal gap between the choices and facts is simply an illusion of human consciousness. Here the term "futurefactuals" is really a misnomer because such truths are only future from the perspective of observers left on the timeline to the event the fact describes. But all points on the timeline eternally exist and are equally real, such that futurefactuals are in fact timeless truths.[31] It is important to stress that the first horn of Swenson's dilemma is essentially an argument that unless the B-Theory of time is true,

---

26. Swenson, "Dilemma," 14:53—15:00.
27. Swenson, "Dilemma," 15:05–30.
28. Swenson, "Dilemma," 15:30–35.
29. Swenson concedes as much: "I say that if a proposition or property (rather than Jones's choice) is the bearer of the explanatory relation, then this removes Jones's control over the situation and undermines his freedom" ("Ability," 667).
30. Swenson, "Ability," 666.
31. Craig, *Divine Foreknowledge*, 14.

Critiquing Explanatory Priority Arguments against Molinism

fatalism is true. Any A-Theorist who denies fatalism should therefore reject the problematic nature of the first horn of Swenson's dilemma.

On the other hand, suppose we answer in the affirmative, saying "Swenson's choice to lie explains L." Swenson supposes that God puts him in C because God knows L and God wants him to lie.[32] For charity's sake, we shall assume that C is one of those rare circumstances, such as Jews being hidden in the basement of a German home during the Nazi era and the Gestapo at the door asking whether Jews are harbored there, where lying is the morally right thing to do. Swenson then claims we get the vicious explanatory loop which I picture in Figure 1.[33]

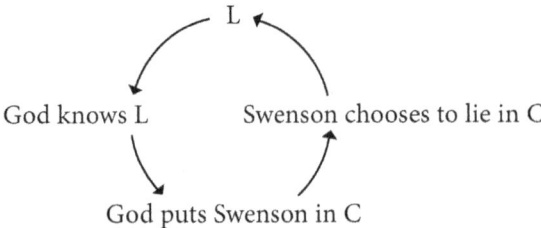

Figure 1

As Flint observes, the only way the loop is vicious is if each arrow (standing for "at least partially explains") means the same thing and if the resulting relation is transitive. Neither of these factors are met.[34] The arrow between "L" and "God knows L" denotes noetic priority, "where to say that X is noetically prior to Y is just to say that Y asserts that someone knows X."[35] Notice that noetic priority designates a necessary and at least roughly sufficient relation. Obviously if L is false, then God cannot know it. If L is true and the God of perfect being theology exists, then God knows L. I say

---

32. Swenson, "Dilemma," 19:44—20:28.

33. Swenson, "Dilemma," 20:28-47; 21:25—22:28. Ironically, this alleged loop was first explicitly developed by neither Adams nor Hasker but by Flint (*Divine Providence*, 159-61; he provides a similar loop image at 160), who formulated it by taking Adams' argument one step further than he did. Flint then proceeds to show that the alleged loop breaks down in various respects (*Divine Providence*, 173-74). Apparently, Swenson does not feel that the loop suffers from the same flaws as its formulator but regards it as a good argument against Molinism.

34. Flint, *Divine Providence*, 173-74.

35. Flint, *Divine Providence*, 173.

"at least roughly sufficient" because the truth of L alone does not imply that God knows L. For L's truth is perfectly compatible with atheism, in which case it is false that God knows L. The arrow between "God knows L" and "God puts Swenson in C" denotes "a partial *reason* for."[36] This is neither a necessary nor a sufficient relation. Regarding lack of necessity, even if God did not know L, God could still put Swenson in C. Adherents of simple foreknowledge (such as Swenson) and open theists insist on this point. Regarding lack of sufficiency, even if God knows L and wants Swenson to lie, God does not have to put Swenson in C. For God possesses libertarian freedom and is thus not constrained by his desires. God can simply choose to act contrary to his desire at this stage.[37]

The arrow between "God puts Swenson in C" and "Swenson chooses to lie in C" denotes "*an enabling condition*," which is at least roughly necessary but not sufficient.[38] If God does not put Swenson in C and Swenson could not have gotten into C without God placing him there, then Swenson would have no opportunity to lie in C.[39] I say "at least roughly necessary" because God's not placing Swenson in C does not itself imply that Swenson did not get into C some other way (on atheism or on a weaker model of divine providence, he could be in C purely by chance), in which case Swenson could still choose to lie in C. Had the antecedent read "Swenson is in C," then the necessity would be strict. But God's putting Swenson in C is not enough to guarantee that Swenson chooses to lie in C. For C represents a freedom-preserving set of circumstances, and Swenson could use his libertarian freedom to either lie or not lie in C. The arrow between "Swenson chooses to lie in C" and "L" denotes genuine counterfactual power over, which is a necessary and sufficient relation. If Swenson chooses not to lie in C, then L is false, and if Swenson chooses to lie in C, then L is true. So we see that each arrow does not mean the same thing as the other arrows and that at least three different functions exist among the arrows, namely, necessity coupled with at least rough sufficiency, at least rough necessity without sufficiency, and neither necessity nor sufficiency. This is enough to show that the loop is not vicious but is held together only in appearance through equivocation of terms.[40]

36. Flint, *Divine Providence*, 173.
37. Flint, *Divine Providence*, 173.
38. Flint, *Divine Providence*, 173.
39. Flint, *Divine Providence*, 173.
40. Flint, *Divine Providence*, 173–74.

Critiquing Explanatory Priority Arguments against Molinism

But let us take the critique one step further: is the resulting relation transitive? Plantinga reveals that the answer is no. Let M stand for the fact that I would mow my lawn in S, where S represents the complete set of circumstances leading up to the moment of my freely mowing last Saturday, and let W stand for the actual world. Let us suppose that one of the reasons God creates W is because God wants me to mow my lawn on the day we now call last Saturday. Recall that the relation under investigation (designated by the arrow) includes noetic priority, a partial reason for, an enabling condition, and genuine counterfactual power over. To borrow and slightly modify Plantinga's example, we find what I illustrate in Figure 2.[41]

Figure 2

The arrow linking "I mowed my lawn last Saturday" to "M" denotes genuine counterfactual power over. The arrow linking "M" to "God knows M" denotes noetic priority. The arrow linking "God knows M" to "God creates W" denotes a partial reason for. The arrow linking "God creates W" to "The Allies won World War II" denotes an enabling condition. For W includes the complete set of circumstances leading up to the moment the Allies freely won World War II. One may here protest that the arrow denotes more than an enabling condition, as God's creating W is sufficient for the Allies winning World War II. But what type of sufficiency is this? It is epistemic sufficiency, where our knowledge that God creates W leads us to validly infer that the Allies win World War II. However, epistemic sufficiency is not the type of sufficiency with which we are concerned here. We are interested in causal sufficiency, namely, whether God's creating W

41. Plantinga, "Reply to Adams," 376.

entails that the Allies *necessarily* win World War II. And the answer is no: God's creating W only entails that the Allies *contingently* win World War II (as is in fact the case), such that they could have lost the war. So the arrow is indeed correctly understood as enabling. Now if the relation under investigation were transitive, my mowing my lawn last Saturday would at least partially explain the Allies winning World War II, which is absurd. By *reductio*, then, the relation is not transitive.[42]

Swenson's Second Argument against Molinism: Divine Intention

Aware of Flint's criticism of the vicious loop,[43] Swenson makes a second argument against Molinism based on the unchangeability of a divine intention. This intention is IG ≡ "God intends to make sure that whoever is in circumstance C tells a lie."[44] Assuming God has IG, Swenson reasons that God "would only put me in C if I would freely tell a lie."[45] But then Swenson supposes that "God's having IG is not explained by facts about what I would freely do in C."[46] However, any Molinist would regard this assumption as false. We already know from the attempted loop that Swenson counts noetic priority as a type of explanation. But Molinism holds that God's middle knowledge (i.e., his prevolitional knowledge of CCFs) informs God's intentions. Hence God's having IG is, on Swenson's understanding, explained by facts about what Swenson would freely do in C. This brings us back to the fallacious loop. However, let us overlook this flaw for the time being and examine the remainder of the argument.

Swenson argues:

1. If I can do anything other than lie, then I can do something incompatible with God's having IG.

2. But . . . I cannot do anything incompatible with God's having IG.

3. Therefore I cannot do anything other than lie.[47]

---

42. Plantinga, "Reply to Adams," 376.
43. Swenson, "Dilemma," 41:12–26.
44. Swenson, "Dilemma," 29:08–48.
45. Swenson, "Dilemma," 29:48–56.
46. Swenson, "Dilemma," 28:40—29:07.
47. Swenson, "Dilemma," 30:11–46.

Critiquing Explanatory Priority Arguments against Molinism

However, premise 1 is false. If Swenson tells the truth, he is not doing anything incompatible with the fact of God's having IG. Swenson is simply frustrating the intention (IG) itself. This is not ruled out by the Fixity of the Independent, which deals with not being able to "do anything incompatible with *facts*"—not *intentions*—"that are not even partially explained by A's choice at time *t*."[48] Whenever we sin, we frustrate God's intentions. So frustrating God's intentions can and is often done. Consequently, Swenson's argument fails even if we grant his dubious assumption.

With Swenson's definition of explanatory priority and arguments against Molinism found wanting, we now turn to a different conception of explanatory priority and a different anti-Molinist argument offered by Climenhaga and Rubio.

Climenhaga and Rubio: Influence and Full Explanation

Climenhaga and Rubio understand the explanatory priority of X to Y in terms of influence. They write, "if X is prior to Y, then X is one of the facts that influences whether Y is true."[49] However, they do not go so far as to define X's priority to Y as X's being among the facts that influence whether Y is true (in other words, they do not write "X is prior to Y iff . . ."). If they did, then their definition would fall prey to Craig's criticism of Hasker's definition. In other words, suppose a symbiotic relationship exists between X and Y such that X influences whether Y is true and Y simultaneously influences whether X is true. To illustrate, a wife's loving her husband influences whether her husband loves her, and this husband's loving his wife simultaneously influences whether his wife loves him. If X's explanatory priority to Y ≡ X's being among the facts that influence whether Y is true, then the relation could only be transitive at the cost of being symmetric and reflexive, so rendering it of no explanatory value.[50] Now Climenhaga and Rubio insist that their "explanatory priority relation is transitive, asymmetric, and irreflexive."[51] So one wonders what more goes into the relation than X's being among the facts that influence whether Y is true. Unfortunately, Climenhaga and Rubio do not say. However, they maintain that "explanatory priority is necessary but not sufficient for explanation. For example,

---

48. Swenson, "Dilemma," 8:28–38, emphasis added.
49. Climenhaga and Rubio, "Molinism," 461.
50. Craig, "Hasker's Defense," 237–38.
51. Climenhaga and Rubio, "Molinism," 461.

Molinist Philosophical and Theological Ventures

the fact that Sally smokes is prior to the fact that she does not get lung cancer, because it is one of the factors that influences whether or not she gets lung cancer. But it does not even partly explain that fact."[52] This admission is crucial because Climenhaga and Rubio, unlike Swenson, concede that partial explanation of a proposed free act is not enough to subvert human freedom; only a full explanation of that act which does not include the person's actually making the choice to perform the act suffices to do so.[53]

Consequently, Climenhaga and Rubio move at this juncture to the notion of full explanation, which they define in terms of determination: "To say that a set of facts Γ fully explains Y is to say that Γ *determines* Y, or *makes it the case that* Y."[54] They further contend that "if Molinism is true, then there is some set of facts Γ that fully explains," i.e., determines, every action.[55] But this is simply mistaken. As abstract objects and thus causally impotent, facts cannot determine actions. Rather, the correspondence theory of truth maintains that reality, including actions and events, determines facts. Climenhaga and Rubio wrongly conflate determination with logical entailment: "If all members of a set of contingent facts Γ are explanatorily prior to Y, and ancestors of Γ only influence Y by influencing Γ, then *if* Γ *entails* Y, Γ *fully explains* Y."[56] To determine Y is to render Y necessary and therefore constitutes a modal notion. To logically entail Y is to show that Y is true while implying nothing concerning the modal status of that proposition—Y's truth could either be contingent or necessary. So Γ's entailing Y does not mean that Γ fully explains, i.e., determines, the action described in Y. Climenhaga and Rubio have committed the modal fallacy of confusing the *necessitas consequentiae* with the *necessitas consequentis*. For from the premises $\Box(\Gamma \rightarrow Y)$ (where $\Box$ reads "necessarily") and Γ, they conclude that $\Box Y$. But the only thing that validly follows from these premises is that Y, not that Y is necessary.[57]

---

52. Climenhaga and Rubio, "Molinism," 461.
53. Climenhaga and Rubio, "Molinism," 467.
54. Climenhaga and Rubio, "Molinism," 461.
55. Climenhaga and Rubio, "Molinism," 462.
56. Climenhaga and Rubio, "Molinism," 465, emphasis added.
57. Moreland and Craig, *Philosophical Foundations*, 46.

Critiquing Explanatory Priority Arguments against Molinism

Climenhaga and Rubio's Argument against Molinism: Molinism Precludes Freedom

In reference to the second half of the Genesis creation narrative, Climenhaga and Rubio formulate the following anti-Molinist argument:

1. If Molinism is true, then there is some set of facts Γ that fully explains Eve's sinning and everything Eve does that influences whether she sins.
2. If Γ fully explains S's φ-ing as well as everything S does that influences whether S φ-s, then S does not do φ freely.
3. Therefore, if Molinism is true, Eve does not freely sin.
4. What goes for Eve's sin goes for any action.
5. Therefore, if Molinism is true, there are no free actions.[58]

The controversial premise in this argument is 1. Dubbing God's creative act of will "Creation," Climenhaga and Rubio point out that "Creation is explanatorily prior to Eve's sin, and the CCFs are prior to Creation. Moreover, the CCF, 'Were Eve tempted by a serpent, she would sin', together with God's creating Eve in those circumstances, entails that Eve sins."[59] Assuming *arguendo* that the relevant notion of explanatory priority is cogent (which I doubt), this claim is unproblematic. However, they proceed to make this assertion which implicitly denies the doctrine of agent causation:

> Since Eve's sin is entailed by factors explanatorily prior to it, then either those factors determine Eve's sin, or there is some other full explanation of Eve's sin that includes common influences on both these factors and Eve's sin. The same goes for everything else Eve does. So there is some set of facts that fully explains both Eve's sin and everything Eve does that influences whether she sins.[60]

Agent causation, in Roderick Chisholm's words, means that

> each of us, when we act, is a prime mover unmoved. In doing what we do, we cause certain events to happen, and nothing—or no one—causes us to cause those events to happen. If we are thus prime movers unmoved and if our actions, or those for which we are responsible, are not causally determined, then they are not

---

58. Climenhaga and Rubio, "Molinism," 462–63; steps 4 and 5 are stated by Climenhaga and Rubio but not numbered. They only number steps 1, 2, and 3.

59. Climenhaga and Rubio, "Molinism," 464.

60. Climenhaga and Rubio, "Molinism," 464.

causally determined by our *desires* . . . beliefs, and stimulus situation at any time.[61]

Climenhaga and Rubio rightly point out that the union of either CCFs and Creation or contingent facts about creaturely essences (which explain CCFs) and Creation does imply what Eve will do.[62] But implication or entailment of what Eve will do is not equivalent to Eve doing what she does necessarily. *À la* Chisholm, no prior conditions, whether {Creation, CCFs} or {Creation, Contingent Facts about Creaturely Essences}, cause Eve to cause her sin; she as a free agent is an unmoved mover and thus the only cause of her sin. However, Climenhaga and Rubio maintain that the union of {Creation, CCFs} and "the (possibly empty) set of all common influences on {Creation, CCFs} and Eve's actions," "must be a *full* explanation, for otherwise we cannot account for Γ *entailing* Y, and not merely probabilifying it."[63] Recalling that full explanation refers to determination, this is a *non sequitur*. For the distinction between entailment and high probability is one between certainty and likelihood, not one between necessity and contingency. Certainty and likelihood are epistemic notions indicating how sure we are that something is true. Necessity and contingency are modal notions indicating whether a proposition is, respectively, not possibly false or possibly false.[64] Certainty and likelihood refer to knowers; necessity and contingency refer to propositions.

Indeed any valid and sound deductive argument will entail its conclusion, or show the conclusion to be true with certainty. By contrast, any strong and cogent inductive argument will probabilify its conclusion, or show the conclusion to be likely but not certainly true. Now a contingent truth can be certainly true, and a necessary truth can be only epistemically probably true. Regarding the former, I know that if I were to offer my wife a glass of Dr Pepper and a glass of Pepsi, then she would choose the glass of Dr Pepper. Suppose that I will make my wife this offer tonight. The conjunction of these premises entail that my wife will choose the glass of Dr

61. Chisholm, "Human Freedom," 434–35.

62. Climenhaga and Rubio, "Molinism," 465–66.

63. Climenhaga and Rubio, "Molinism," 466, 467.

64. Craig observes: "In the writings of contemporary theological fatalists, one frequently finds statements which slide from affirming that something is *certainly* true to affirming that something is *necessarily* true. This is sheer confusion. Certainty is a property of persons . . . by contrast, necessity is a property of statements or propositions. . . . Thus, when we say that some statement is 'certainly true,' this is but a manner of speaking indicating that we are certain the statement is true" ("Middle-Knowledge View," 127).

Pepper tonight, such that her doing so is certainly true. In other words, I am 100 percent sure that she will choose the glass of Dr Pepper. However, does my epistemic state or the syllogism that furnished me with that state do anything to necessitate that my wife chooses the glass of Dr Pepper, exerting irresistible causal power over her will? Of course not; she chooses the glass of Dr Pepper contingently (she could have done otherwise), and her so choosing is simply a matter of her free will. Regarding the latter, let us take a mathematical theorem whose truth we can give very good reasons for but cannot prove. The conjunction of these reasons yield an inductive argument for the theorem which render it epistemically probably true. However, if it is true, it is true in all possible worlds and is therefore necessarily true.

Returning to the example about my wife, even though the conjunction of the relevant premises entail my wife choosing the glass of Dr Pepper, those premises do not constitute a full explanation. A full explanation requires the actual act of my wife's free decision, which is missing from the premises. Thus we have, on this example, a partial explanation. The same is true with Eve's sin and with any other action. Climenhaga and Rubio seem to realize this later in their article when they write, "what undermines freedom is not explanatorily prior facts that entail an action, but explanatorily prior facts that fully explain an action."[65] But they insist that in the case of Eve, they possess a full explanation. They maintain that this full explanation could come about in one of two ways: CCFs being immediately explanatorily prior to Eve's sin, or contingent facts about creaturely essences being immediately explanatorily prior to Eve's sin.

Let us consider the first possibility: are CCFs immediately explanatorily prior to Eve's sin? Recall that, according to Climenhaga and Rubio, a prerequisite for CCFs to play this role is for them to influence whether Eve in fact sins. But on agent causation, which Molinism assumes, they do not exert any influence upon Eve's actual sinning. While CCFs are true chronologically prior to Eve's sin, they are invisible to Eve's sin. Eve sins just as freely as she would if there were no CCFs true temporally before her sin. There simply exists an acausal, i.e., noninfluential, symmetry between the relevant CCF and Eve's sin. To think, as Climenhaga and Rubio do, that this symmetry indicates a relationship of influence is, in Craig's words, to "mistakenly assimilat[e] the semantic relation between a true proposition and the corresponding actual state of affairs to the causal relation."[66]

---

65. Climenhaga and Rubio, "Molinism," 476.
66. Craig, *Divine Foreknowledge*, 261.

Accordingly, the acausal symmetry between the relevant CCF and Eve's sin is merely a semantic relation, and there exists no explanatory arrow from CCFs to Eve's sin.

We shall now consider whether contingent facts about creaturely essences are immediately explanatorily prior to Eve's sin. Here Climenhaga and Rubio make the critical assumption that "Eve does not do anything to influence the contingent facts about her essence. So it seems like a matter of luck that the contingent facts about Eve's essence are what they are. And if this is the case, it seems like a matter of luck that Eve acts in the way determined by those facts."[67] However, philosophers who believe that contingent facts about creaturely essences serve as truthmakers for CCFs also believe that, in John Laing's words, "the creaturely wills which pre-exist in the divine mind as ideas" constitute the source of those contingent facts.[68] Thus Eve's preexistent will yields the contingent facts about her essence, rather than the facts determining her will or the facts being simply a matter of luck. Hence there is no explanatory arrow from contingent facts about creaturely essences to Eve's sin. Of course, the Molinist is free to deny that contingent facts about one's essence exist, as there are many other ways of dispensing with the grounding objection. If, as I suggest, divinely intuited beliefs about individual creaturely essences ground CCFs, then they do not stand in any chain connected to CCFs because truthmaking is not a causal, namely influential, relation.

Conclusion

The refurbished versions of the Adams-Hasker argument offered by Swenson, Climenhaga, and Rubio have been examined and found wanting. Swenson's version of explanatory priority is both equivocal and intransitive, and his principle of the Fixity of the Independent is either incoherent, false, or trivially true. It is trivially true if we concede that genuine counterfactual power is explanatory, which renders the principle consonant with Molinism. We have seen that Swenson's dilemma against Molinism furnishes no defeater to Molinism. If we take the first horn of the dilemma, claiming that the CCFs regarding our actual choices are not explained by our choices, then we can still do otherwise than the CCFs state. It is simply that we contingently will not. If we take the second horn of the dilemma, claiming that

67. Climenhaga and Rubio, "Molinism," 481.
68. Laing, "Molinism and Supercomprehension," 338.

Critiquing Explanatory Priority Arguments against Molinism

the CCFs regarding our actual choices are explained by our choices, this does not result in a vicious explanatory loop because the "at least partially explains" locution is equivocal and intransitive. Neither does Swenson's divine intention argument against Molinism yield a defeater because it mistakenly assumes that God's intentions are logically prior to God's middle knowledge and that free creatures cannot frustrate God's intentions.

Climenhaga and Rubio's definition of explanatory priority only furnishes a necessary but not sufficient condition for priority and is therefore impossible to verify. In any case, their notion that full explanation, or determination, results when every member of a set of contingent facts stands explanatorily prior to an event and facts influencing this set do not directly impact the event, commits the fallacy of confusing the *necessitas consequentiae* with the *necessitas consequentis*. While this set of contingent facts entails that the event will happen, it does not imply that the event will happen necessarily. Consequently, Climenhaga and Rubio's argument that Molinism precludes human freedom fails to make the crucial distinction between certainty (an epistemic notion resulting from entailment) and necessity (a modal notion resulting from causal determinism). Their suggestion that CCFs stand immediately prior to our actions is dubious because the CCFs are causally indeterminative. Further, their suggestion that contingent facts about creaturely essences stand immediately explanatorily prior to our actions is dubious because, if there are such contingent facts, they emanate from the preexistent creaturely wills in the mind of God.

As a result, no explanatory priority argument against Molinism seems sound. By contrast, analysis of these arguments enables us to amplify and defend crucial features of the Molinist account.

5

A Molinist Interpretation of Alleged Open Theist Prooftexts

IN SUPPORT OF THEIR claim that God lacks knowledge of true counterfactuals of creaturely freedom (CCFs), open theists appeal to biblical passages depicting God as changing plans or learning facts as a result of his relationship to creatures. Prominent among such texts are assertions that God faces situations different than or contrary to what he had anticipated (Isa 5:2–5; 63:8–10; Jer 3:3–20; 7:31; 32:35; Ezek 22:30–31), tests creatures to discover the level of their allegiance to him (Gen 22:12; Deut 8:2–21; 13:1–3; Judg 3:4; 2 Chr 32:31), "changes his mind" (Exod 32:9–14; Isa 38:1–5; Jer 18:4–11; 26:7–19; Joel 2:12–13; Jonah 3:9—4:2), and "repents of" or "regrets" choices he himself made (Gen 6:6; 1 Sam 13:13; 15:10, 35; 1 Chr 21:15).[1]

Although these texts are frequently interpreted by exegetes as anthropomorphisms, or metaphors describing God in human terms, open theists object that in this case no literal truths exist to which these passages point, hence rendering the passages meaningless. Distinguishing the aforementioned texts from such obvious anthropomorphisms as God's having physical features, Gregory Boyd declares:

> Expressions like "the right hand of God" or "the eyes of the Lord," for example, communicate something true of God's strength and knowledge. But what does the concept of God's changing his mind

1. MacGregor, *Systematic Theology*, 91.

A Molinist Interpretation of Alleged Open Theist Prooftexts

communicate, for example, if indeed it is an anthropomorphism? If God in fact never changes his mind, saying he does so doesn't communicate anything truthful: it is simply inaccurate.[2]

Since God, open theists contend, cannot display cognitive changeability or growth in his relationships with creatures if he already knew everything they would do, God must not possess knowledge of CCFs if biblical infallibility is true.[3]

In this piece I will take up Boyd's challenge. Regarding texts that depict God as confronting unexpected situations, testing people, and changing his mind, I will argue that such passages are metaphorical and that Molinism discloses the literal truths to which these passages point. Regarding texts that depict God as regretting decisions, I will argue that such passages can be construed either metaphorically or literally. If these passages are metaphorical, Molinism discloses the literal truths to which they point. If these passages are literal, Molinism explains how they can be literally true.[4]

The Logical Structure of Natural Knowledge and Intrinsic Probabilities

Because God is, among other things, the supremely logical and rational mind, his knowledge can be heuristically subdivided into logical moments, as Molinism has done. But now the question arises: where should God's knowledge of "would probably" counterfactuals be placed in the Molinist scheme? I propose that "would probably" counterfactuals are statements of possibility which are intrinsically more likely to occur than not under the specified circumstances. The proposition "*P* would probably freely perform *a* in *C*" is thus logically equivalent to the proposition "The intrinsic probability that *P* freely performs *a* in *C* is greater than ½."

I further propose that "would probably" counterfactuals belong to God's natural knowledge rather than middle knowledge. We recall that the intrinsic probability of a proposition, according to Richard Swinburne,

---

2. Boyd, "Open-Theism View," 39.
3. MacGregor, *Systematic Theology*, 92.
4. In my earlier work, I presented Boyd's challenge and made a first attempt to take up his challenge to explain these texts (MacGregor, *Systematic Theology*, 90–107). However, I have since changed my view of these texts considerably and no longer regard my first attempt as accurate. Hence this piece explains the same texts as I attempted to previously explain in what I consider a much more plausible and satisfying way.

is its "prior probability arising from its content alone and independent of all evidence."[5] Moreover, Swinburne has effectively argued that every proposition necessarily possesses an intrinsic probability.[6] As metaphysically necessary truths, the intrinsic probability (P) of every logically possible proposition (e.g., P(P freely performs *a* in C) = .6), and the "would probably" counterfactuals derivable from them, belong to God's natural knowledge. Thus every counterfactual of creaturely freedom necessarily has an intrinsic probability. If God has middle knowledge, which includes prevolitional knowledge of at least all true counterfactuals of creaturely freedom,[7] then middle knowledge affords decisive evidence for or against every counterfactual of creaturely freedom. The conditional probability of any counterfactual of creaturely freedom given that it is middle-known by God is 1, and the conditional probability of any counterfactual of creaturely freedom given that it is not middle-known by God is 0. Hence this analysis furnishes two independent grounds for locating "would probably" counterfactuals in God's natural knowledge: they are metaphysically necessary truths; and they are conceptually prior to the contents of middle knowledge. What David Werther observed about "might" counterfactuals equally applies to "would probably" counterfactuals: they "are rightly classed, along with all other necessary truths, among God's natural knowledge. And this, I take it, is the reason why classical Molinism never included these sorts of counterfactuals among God's middle knowledge."[8]

Extending Werther's hunch about "might" counterfactuals to "would probably" counterfactuals regarding classical Molinism appears to be on

---

5. Swinburne, *Epistemic Justification*, 138n12.

6. Swinburne, *Epistemic Justification*, 110–15.

7. I say "at least" because middle knowledge may also include all true counterfactuals of natural randomness, i.e., counterfactual truths about indeterminate natural processes (MacGregor, *Molina*, 92–96).

8. Werther, "Open Theism," 13. I also construe "might" counterfactuals as statements of intrinsic probability. Thus "*P* might freely perform *a* in *C*" is logically equivalent to the proposition "The intrinsic probability that *P* freely performs *a* in *C* is greater than some very low probability (.1, say)." This accords well with Moreland and Craig's depiction of "might" counterfactuals: "'Might' counterfactuals should not be confused with subjunctive conditionals involving the world 'could.' 'Could' is taken to express mere possibility and so is a constituent of a modal statement expressing a possible truth. The distinction is important because the fact that something could happen under certain circumstances does not imply that it might happen under those circumstances. 'Might' is more restrictive than 'could' and indicates a genuine, live option under the circumstances, not a bare logical possibility" (*Philosophical Foundations*, 47).

A Molinist Interpretation of Alleged Open Theist Prooftexts

point. Although Molina never explicitly discussed "would probably" counterfactuals, it seems the only way to render Molina's thought self-consistent is to assume that he classified them as belonging to God's natural knowledge. Molina recognized that the objects God knows with certainty in his middle knowledge are in themselves (*in se*) and in their own right (*secundum se*) uncertain, i.e., they are intrinsically uncertain.[9] Thus Molina wrote, "We claim that the certitude of this middle knowledge has *its* source, in turn, in the depth and unlimited perfection of the divine intellect, a perfection by which God knows with certainty what is in itself uncertain."[10] Again, Molina claimed that the certainty of middle knowledge "flows from the depth and from the infinite and unlimited perfection of the knower, who *in Himself* knows with certainty an object that *in its own right* is uncertain and deceptive."[11] Molina's remark that these objects are "deceptive" is telling. For it implies that these objects—these CCFs—often possess truth values that are contraindicated by their intrinsic probabilities. In other words, some of these objects describe things that would occur despite their being intrinsically unlikely, and some of these objects describe things that would not occur despite their being intrinsically likely. But then the question presses: when in the logical order does God know these intrinsic probabilities? Clearly an omniscient God must know these facts, facts which Molina himself tacitly recognized. Since middle knowledge affords God certainty regarding CCFs, certainty given which the probability of each CCF is either 1 or 0, it follows that God knew the intrinsic probability of each CCF logically beforehand, namely, in his natural knowledge.

Accordingly, within God's natural knowledge is either the proposition "*P* would probably freely perform *a* in *C*" (if the intrinsic probability of *P*'s performing *a* in *C* is greater than ½) or the proposition "*P* would probably not freely perform *a* in *C*" (if the intrinsic probability of *P*'s performing *a* in *C* is less than or equal to ½). And God's middle knowledge that *P* would or would not freely perform *a* in *C* is logically posterior to what God knows would probably or would not probably be the case. The fact that often "would probably" propositions are correlated with "would not" results and often "would probably not" propositions are correlated with "would" results is not a matter of God's natural knowledge containing false beliefs. For the "would probably" and "would probably not" propositions

9. Molina, *Foreknowledge*, 157n18.
10. Molina, *Foreknowledge*, 248 (4.53.10).
11. Molina, *Foreknowledge*, 157 (4.51.18).

are true, accurately expressing intrinsic probabilities. Rather, it is simply testimony to the fact that often intrinsically improbable events would and do occur, and intrinsically probable events would and do fail to occur. We may now apply these insights to the four categories of texts appealed to by open theists.

1. Molinist Interpretation of Texts Depicting Divine Confrontation of the Unexpected

Texts depicting God's confrontation of unexpected situations may readily be interpreted as metaphors of either of two literal truths. One, God's knowledge that some events would happen was logically preceded by God's knowledge that those events possessed an intrinsic probability less than or equal to ½ (i.e., that they would probably not happen). Two, God's knowledge that some events would not happen was logically preceded by God's knowledge that those events possessed an intrinsic probability greater than ½ (i.e., that they would probably happen).

As an illustration of the first case we may use Jeremiah 32:35, which quotes God as saying to Judah, "They built the high places of Baal in the valley of the son of Hinnom, to offer up their sons and daughters to Molech, though I did not command them, nor did it enter my mind that they should do this abomination." This text metaphorically depicts the literal truth that, in the logical order of things, God's (natural) knowledge that the people of Judah's offering their children to Molech was intrinsically improbable (i.e., that they would probably not offer the children) came before God's (middle) knowledge that Judah would offer the children to Molech. The specific language "nor did it enter my mind" further metaphorically indicates that the intrinsic probability of the people's offering their children to Molech was extremely low.

As an illustration of the second case we may use Jeremiah 3:19–20, which quotes God as saying to Israel, "I thought how I would set you among my children, and give you a pleasant land, the most beautiful heritage of all the nations. And I thought you would call me, My Father, and would not turn from following me. Instead, as a faithless wife leaves her husband, so you have been faithless to me, O house of Israel." This text metaphorically depicts the literal truth that, in the logical order of things, God's (natural) knowledge that Israel's remaining faithful to God was intrinsically more probable than not (i.e., that Israel would probably

A Molinist Interpretation of Alleged Open Theist Prooftexts

remain faithful to God) came before God's (middle) knowledge that Israel would prove unfaithful to God.

2. Molinist Interpretation of Texts Depicting Divine Testing of Human Character

Texts depicting God's testing of human character may readily be interpreted as God's placing persons in circumstances, concerning which his knowledge of the intrinsic improbability of persons' obeying his will therein logically preceded his knowledge that persons would or would not disobey his will therein. Here Job 1:9–12 is instructive:

> Then Satan answered the LORD, "Does Job fear God for nothing? Have you not put a fence around him and his house and all that he has, on every side? You have blessed the work of his hands, and his possessions have increased in the land. But stretch out your hand now, and touch all that he has, and he will curse you to your face." The LORD said to Satan, "Very well, all that he has is in your power; only do not stretch out your hand against him!" So Satan went out from the presence of the LORD.

Here Satan presents God with the intrinsic improbability of Job's remaining faithful to God if Job lost his property and children, an improbability that Satan presumably assesses accurately because God did not correct him. Later we learn that Job proved faithful: "Then Job arose, tore his robe, shaved his head, and fell on the ground and worshiped. He said, 'Naked I came from my mother's womb, and naked shall I return there; the LORD gave, and the LORD has taken away; blessed be the name of the LORD.' In all this Job did not sin or charge God with wrongdoing" (Job 1:20–22). Hence Job 1 metaphorically presents us with the literal truth that God placed Job in circumstances where he would lose his property and children, circumstances concerning which God's (natural) knowledge that the intrinsic probability of Job's cursing God to his face logically preceded God's (middle) knowledge that Job would not sin.

The most widely known testing passage in Scripture occurs in Genesis 22, where God makes the extraordinary request of Abraham that he sacrifice Isaac on Mount Moriah. However, once Abraham takes out the knife for the sacrifice, God stops Isaac's death through this command: "Do not lay your hand on the boy or do anything to him; for now I know that you fear God, since you have not withheld your son, your only son, from me" (Gen 22:12). God's statement that "now I know that you fear God" is a temporal metaphor for the literal truth that God's (natural) knowledge of the intrinsic improbability of Abraham's obeying the divine command to sacrifice Isaac logically preceded God's (middle) knowledge that Abraham would attempt to obey the command.

3. Molinist Interpretation of Texts Depicting Divine Changes of Mind

Texts depicting God's changing his mind may readily be interpreted as metaphors for the fact that what God chooses to do in his divine creative decree is contraindicated by the expectation of what God would do in the relevant scenario based on God's natural knowledge of various intrinsic probabilities.[12] Let us first consider the golden calf incident, where God's chosen people break their promise to observe the Mosaic Covenant through blatant acts of idolatry and debauchery. When the Israelites worship the golden calf, Exodus 32:9–14 narrates the following conversation between God and Moses:

> The LORD said to Moses, "I have seen this people, how stiff-necked they are. Now let me alone, so that my wrath may burn hot against them and I may consume them; and of you I will make a great nation." But Moses implored the LORD his God, and said, "O LORD, why does your wrath burn hot against your people, whom you brought out of the land of Egypt with great power and with a mighty hand? Why should the Egyptians say, 'It was with evil intent that he brought them out to kill them in the mountains, and to consume them from the face of the earth'? Turn from your fierce wrath; change your mind and do not bring disaster on your people. Remember Abraham, Isaac, and Israel, your servants, how you swore to them by your own self, saying to them, 'I will multiply your descendants like the stars of heaven, and all this land that I have promised I will give to your descendants, and they shall inherit it forever.'" And the LORD changed his mind about the disaster that he planned to bring on his people.[13]

---

12. We may thus say that the relevant true counterfactual of divine freedom known to God in his free knowledge is contraindicated by the associated true "would probably" counterfactual known to God in his natural knowledge.

13. I owe my subsequent exegesis of this pericope to the comments of an anonymous reviewer.

A Molinist Interpretation of Alleged Open Theist Prooftexts

Let C (variable choice based on the word "calf") be the proposition "The children of Israel betray God by making and worshiping the golden calf." Let W (variable choice based on the word "wrath") be the proposition "God informs Moses of God's fierce wrath toward the Israelites." Let E (variable choice based on the word "entreat") be the proposition "Moses entreats God for the people's deliverance." Let D (variable choice based on the word "destroy") be the proposition "God destroys the people." Suppose God knows in his natural knowledge the following intrinsic probabilities (the $\Box\!\!\rightarrow$ operator stands for "if the antecedent were the case, then the consequent would be the case"):

1. $P((C \ \& \ W \ \& \sim E) \ \Box\!\!\rightarrow D) = .9$
2. $P((C \ \& \ W \ \& \ E) \ \Box\!\!\rightarrow \sim D) = .9$
3. $P((C \ \& \ W) \ \Box\!\!\rightarrow E) = .1$

Hence God knows, logically prior to his middle knowledge and hence prior to making any creative decision, the high intrinsic probability that God would destroy the Israelites if the Israelites were to worship the golden calf, God were to tell Moses of God's fierce wrath toward the Israelites, and Moses were not to entreat God for the people's deliverance (by knowing 1) as well as the high intrinsic probability that God wouldn't destroy the Israelites if the Israelites were to worship the golden calf, God were to inform Moses of God's fierce wrath toward the Israelites, and Moses were to entreat God for the people's deliverance (by knowing 2). But God also knows in his natural knowledge the low intrinsic probability of Moses' entreating God for the people's deliverance if the Israelites were to worship the golden calf and God were to inform Moses of his fierce wrath toward the Israelites. In view of this situation, at the stage of natural knowledge the expectation exists that God would destroy the Israelites under the relevant circumstances.[14] To express this truth, the Bible describes God's informing Moses of his fierce wrath toward the Israelites with the metaphor that God tells Moses he will destroy the Israelites under the relevant circumstances. (We may also add that this metaphor accurately describes what Moses actually deduced God would do based on the communication of his fierce wrath. It is how Moses interpreted God's communication.) However, in God's middle knowledge, God perceives that (C & W) $\Box\!\!\rightarrow$ E (i.e., if the Israelites were

---

14. Thus God knows, in his natural knowledge, the true counterfactual "God would probably destroy the Israelites under the relevant circumstances."

Molinist Philosophical and Theological Ventures

to worship the golden calf and God were to tell Moses of his fierce wrath toward them, then Moses would entreat God for their deliverance) is true, despite the overwhelming odds against it. This logically posterior knowledge along with God's subsequent decision to create the scenario where the Israelites worship the golden calf, God tells Moses of his fierce wrath toward them, Moses entreats God for their deliverance, and God spares the people is depicted by the biblical metaphor that God changed his mind.[15]

Likewise, we reflect on the account of Hezekiah's illness in Isaiah 38:1–5:

> In those days Hezekiah became sick and was at the point of death. The prophet Isaiah son of Amoz came to him, and said to him, "Thus says the LORD: Set your house in order, for you shall die; you shall not recover." Then Hezekiah turned his face to the wall, and prayed to the LORD: "Remember now, O LORD, I implore you, how I have walked before you in faithfulness with a whole heart, and have done what is good in your sight." And Hezekiah wept bitterly. Then the word of the LORD came to Isaiah: "Go and say to Hezekiah, Thus says the LORD, the God of your ancestor David: I have heard your prayer, I have seen your tears; I will add fifteen years to your life."

Let S (variable choice based on the word "sickness") be the proposition "Hezekiah degenerates in sickness to the brink of death." Let A (variable choice based on the word "advised") be the proposition "Isaiah advises Hezekiah to set his house in order." Let I (variable choice based on the word "implored") be the proposition "Hezekiah implores God for a longer life." Let E (variable choice based on the word "extend") be the proposition "God extends Hezekiah's life by fifteen years." Suppose God knows in his natural knowledge the following intrinsic probabilities:

1. $P((S \& A \& \sim I) \Box\!\!\rightarrow \sim E) = .9$
2. $P((S \& A \& I) \Box\!\!\rightarrow E) = .9$
3. $P((S \& A) \Box\!\!\rightarrow I) = .1$

Hence God knows, logically prior to his middle knowledge and hence prior to making any creative decision, the high intrinsic probability that God would allow Hezekiah's natural death if Hezekiah were to become sick

---

15. Thus God knows, in his free knowledge, the true counterfactual "God would not destroy the Israelites under the relevant circumstances," which is contraindicated by the associated true "would probably" counterfactual.

A Molinist Interpretation of Alleged Open Theist Prooftexts

to the point of death, Isaiah were to advise Hezekiah to set his house in order, and Hezekiah were not to implore God for a longer life (by knowing 1) as well as the high intrinsic probability that God would extend Hezekiah's life by fifteen years if Hezekiah were to become sick to the point of death, Isaiah were to advise Hezekiah to set his house in order, and Hezekiah were to implore God for a longer life (by knowing 2). But God also knows in his natural knowledge the low intrinsic probability of Hezekiah's imploring God for a longer life if he were to degenerate in sickness to the brink of death and Isaiah were to advise him to set his house in order. In view of this situation, at the stage of natural knowledge the expectation exists that God would allow Hezekiah's natural death under the relevant circumstances.[16] To express this truth, the Bible describes Isaiah's advising Hezekiah to set his house in order with the metaphor of Isaiah's relating God's word that Hezekiah must set his house in order and will die. (We may also add that this metaphor accurately expresses how Hezekiah interpreted Isaiah's advice, namely, as a divine oracle of Hezekiah's demise.) However, in God's middle knowledge, God perceives that (S & A) $\Box\!\!\rightarrow$ I (i.e., if Hezekiah were to become sick to the point of death and Isaiah were to advise him to set his house in order, then Hezekiah would implore God for a longer life) is true, despite the overwhelming odds against it. This logically posterior knowledge along with God's subsequent decision to create the scenario where Hezekiah becomes sick to the point of death, Isaiah advises Hezekiah to set his house in order, Hezekiah implores God for a longer life, and God extends Hezekiah's life by fifteen years is depicted by the Bible's metaphorical portrayal of God's changing his mind.[17]

4. Molinist Interpretation of Texts Depicting Divine "Repentance" or "Regret" for Decisions Made

Texts depicting God's "repentance" or "regret" for decisions made may be interpreted either metaphorically or literally. If the former, they are metaphors for the fact that God chose, in the divine creative decision, to actualize persons and circumstances for which the "would probably"

---

16. Thus God knows, in his natural knowledge, the true counterfactual "God would probably allow Hezekiah to die a natural death under the relevant circumstances."

17. Thus God knows, in his free knowledge, the true counterfactual "God would extend Hezekiah's life by fifteen years under the relevant circumstances," which is contraindicated by the associated true "would probably" counterfactual.

counterfactual known in natural knowledge suggested a desirable result but where the "would" counterfactual known in middle knowledge turned out to be undesirable. This makes sense of Genesis 6:5–6: "The Lord saw that the wickedness of humankind was great in the earth, and that every inclination of the thoughts of their hearts was only evil continually. And the Lord was sorry that he had made humankind on the earth, and it grieved him to his heart." The "would probably" counterfactual indicated that the intrinsic probability of humankind's remaining at least somewhat righteous in the relevant circumstances was greater than ½. However, the logically subsequent "would" counterfactual disclosed that humankind in those circumstances would descend into complete moral depravity. Nonetheless, God decided to create humankind in those circumstances. Likewise, 1 Samuel 15:11, "I regret that I made Saul king, for he has turned back from following me, and has not carried out my commands," indicates the truth of the counterfactual "If Saul were king in the relevant circumstances, then he would probably follow God and observe God's commands" coupled with the logically subsequent truth of the counterfactual "If Saul were king in the relevant circumstances, then he would neither follow God nor observe God's commands." Nonetheless, God decided to make Saul king in those circumstances. This dissimilarity between the "would probably" and "would" counterfactuals in situations God actualizes is captured in the metaphors of divine sorrow, grief, and repentance.

But these texts may also be interpreted literally. To make this argument, I here propose that middle knowledge afforded God with knowledge of counterfactuals of divine emotion. If God has an emotional life which is known perfectly to him, then God apprehends his emotions concerning CCFs. God knows what his emotions would be if each CCF were actual. In particular, God knows what his emotions would be if he were to actualize various compossible CCFs. Since such knowledge is dependent on God's knowledge of the CCFs' truth, God's knowledge of counterfactuals of divine emotion logically follows his knowledge of the CCFs they are about. However, knowledge of counterfactuals of divine emotion inform, and are thus logically prior to, God's creative decision intervening between his middle and free knowledge. Because God's creative decision is not a moment of knowledge, counterfactuals of divine emotion must be known by God in his middle knowledge. Thus middle knowledge includes knowledge of all CCFs and, logically posterior to them, all counterfactuals of divine emotion.

A Molinist Interpretation of Alleged Open Theist Prooftexts

My proposal clearly assumes the falsity of the doctrine of divine impassibility, or God's "incapacity for or insusceptibility to emotional experiences."[18] Although divine impassibility has constituted a traditional Christian doctrine, the tide of mainstream philosophical and theological opinion has turned largely against this doctrine. As Anastasia Scrutton reports, "The impassibilist consensus remained almost entirely unchallenged until the turn of the twentieth century, from which point *passibilism* increasingly became the predominant position among theologians and philosophers of religion."[19]

Today most theologians find impassibility irreconcilable with the love of God and the witness of Scripture. God's love is not simply the unidirectional relationship of active benevolence toward his creation, but a genuinely bidirectional relationship where God is so intimately involved with his creation that he is emotionally influenced by it. Regarding biblical fidelity, Wayne Grudem observes:

> The idea that God has no passions or emotions *at all* clearly conflicts with . . . Scripture, and for that reason I have not affirmed God's impassibility. . . . Instead, quite the opposite is true, for God, who is the origin of our emotions and who created our emotions, certainly does feel emotions: God rejoices (Isa. 62:5). He is grieved (Ps. 78:40; Eph. 4:30). His wrath burns hot against his enemies (Ex. 32:10). He pities his children (Ps. 103:13). . . . He is a God whose passions we are to imitate for all eternity as we like our Creator hate sin and delight in righteousness.[20]

Gordon Lewis nicely sums up the majority view of contemporary Christian thinkers in these words:

> Just as God perfectly uses his intellectual and volitional powers, he perfectly uses his emotional powers. Negatively, God has . . . no emotions inconsistent with all his other attributes. God is not overcome by emotions, has no emotions out of control, out of balance, or inappropriate to the situation. God does not suffer emotional disorders. Affirmatively, the God of the Bible has an appropriate, healthy, self-controlled emotional experience. As exhibited in Jesus, the Father may be viewed as weeping with those who weep and rejoicing with those who rejoice.[21]

18. Scrutton, "Living," 374.
19. Scrutton, "Living," 374.
20. Grudem, *Systematic Theology*, 166.
21. Lewis, "Impassibility," 422.

Molinist Philosophical and Theological Ventures

But as Kristján Kristjánsson points out, a fully mature and healthy emotional experience includes emotional ambivalence, namely, the fact that a single situation or episode can elicit contrasting, *prima facie* irreconcilable emotions.[22] For example, taking the biblical text literally, God has a love-hate relationship with evildoers, unconditionally loving (Matt 5:44–48) and hating (Pss 5:5; 11:5) them simultaneously. Mikko Salmela underscores that emotional ambivalence is not logically inconsistent because the *prima facie* irreconcilable emotions are grounded in different reasons.[23] Thus God unconditionally loves evildoers on account of their being persons, and he hates evildoers on account of their sin. What would make *prima facie* irreconcilable emotions genuinely irreconcilable is if they were grounded in the same reason, which is never the case with God. Molina held that God, in his free knowledge, possessed knowledge of counterfactuals of divine freedom.[24] For, as part of God's creative decision, God decided what he would do in any conceivable circumstances along with which compossible set of circumstances, or feasible world, he would actualize. This has profound ramifications in view of God's middle knowledge of counterfactuals of divine emotion. God's choice to create a particular world is also a choice to experience a set of emotions associated with that world, a set including emotional ambivalence regarding various circumstances therein. Thus *prima facie* irreconcilable emotions do not surprise God when he feels them in time.

Texts depicting God's "repentance" or "regret" for decisions made may, therefore, be interpreted as literal descriptions of the emotions God experienced in time over certain facets of those decisions. Hence God made certain decisions, knowing logically before making them that he would feel sorry for or regret them for some reasons but also knowing that he would not feel sorry for or regret them for other, more important reasons. In this case, Genesis 6:5–6 would indicate that God literally felt sorry and grief for making humanity on account of their extreme wickedness. However, God simultaneously felt gratified for making humanity on account of the salvation received by those who would freely love him, among other reasons. The latter reasons trump the former reason, leading God to create humanity with logically prior knowledge of the differing emotions this would spur. Such *prima facie* irreconcilable emotions are not contradictory

---

22. Kristjánsson, *Aristotle*, 93.
23. Salmela, *True Emotions*, 115.
24. Flint, *Divine Providence*, 55–57.

because they are grounded in different reasons, and this emotional ambivalence is the mark of the fully mature, healthy emotional experience that God exemplifies.

Likewise, 1 Samuel 15:11 would indicate that God literally regretted making Saul king on account of his unfaithfulness. But God simultaneously felt gratified for making Saul king on account of, among other reasons, the fact that Saul's being king would positively contribute to the world's obtaining an optimal salvific balance. Because the latter reasons outweigh the former reason, God made Saul king, knowing logically prior to deciding upon this action the conflicting emotions it would elicit. Again, such emotional ambivalence is logically consistent and evidences God's perfect emotional stability.

Conclusion

While not discussed by Molina, Molinism provides a conceptual framework which readily accommodates "would probably" counterfactuals. As necessarily true propositions concerning intrinsic probability, "would probably" counterfactuals belong to God's natural knowledge. In view of this, a Molinist exegesis of alleged open theist prooftexts reveal them to be largely if not exclusively temporal metaphors for timeless relations of logical order. Texts depicting God's confrontation of unexpected events metaphorically depict the timeless relation that God's knowledge of the intrinsic probability of events logically precedes God's knowledge that those events would or would not happen, where the intrinsic probability was either less than or equal to ½ though the events would happen or greater than ½ though the events would not happen. Texts depicting God's testing of human character metaphorically depict the timeless relation that God's knowledge that persons' obeying his will in various circumstances had an intrinsic probability less than or equal to ½ came logically prior to God's knowledge that persons would or would not obey his will in those circumstances. Texts depicting God's changing his mind metaphorically depict that God's creative decision to act a certain way in a scenario is contraindicated by the expectation of how God would act in that scenario (i.e., how God would probably act in that scenario) based on God's natural knowledge of various intrinsic probabilities. Texts depicting God's "repentance" or "regret" for various decisions can be interpreted in one of two ways. First, they may metaphorically depict the fact that God chose, in the divine creative decision, to actualize persons and circumstances featuring a desirable "would probably" counterfactual and an undesirable "would" counterfactual. Second, they may be literal depictions of emotions, rooted in various reasons, God experienced for making those decisions and middle-knew he would experience logically before making those decisions. However, those were not the only emotions God experienced and middle-knew he would experience for making those decisions. God middle-knew he would feel other, positive emotions, rooted in superior reasons, for those very same decisions, and these superior reasons led God to make the decisions.

Meeting the challenge laid out by Boyd, then, Molinism enables us to identify the literal truth underlying alleged open theist prooftexts without resorting to open theism.

— 6 —

The Logical Consistency of Molinism on Branching Time Models

The philosophical logician Alex Malpass argues that Molinism is proven logically inconsistent by branching time models in three respects. (1) Given consecutive temporal moments t_n, t_{n+1}, and t_{n+2}, there can be no truth value at t_{n+2} to propositions expressing what, had a different future resulted from an event at t_n, would have eventuated from a nonactual indeterminate event at t_{n+1}.[1] (2) Molinism makes propositions about possible worlds containing compound tenses fail.[2] (3) Branching time models force Molinism to posit the absurdity of two different types of actuality.[3] This chapter argues that none of these objections is true. I show that (1) is based on the false metaphysical assumption that time makes things happen rather than either recording what things happen or being produced by things happening. Thus, while humans cannot know the relevant truth value at t_{n+2}, this does not imply that there is no truth value at t_{n+2}. I show that (2) confuses the actual past (and future) with nonactual pasts (and futures) and that, when these are differentiated, propositions about possible worlds containing compound tenses succeed. Finally, I show that (3) branching time models merely force the Molinist to distinguish possibility, feasibility,

---

1. Malpass, "Grounding Objection," 24:30—36:46.
2. Malpass, "Grounding Objection," 36:51—40:26.
3. Malpass, "Grounding Objection," 40:27—41:56.

and actuality, such that only the feasible world chosen by God is actual. In the process, I illustrate how Molinism is logically consistent with and illuminated by branching time models. Here a caveat is in order. I do not regard branching time models as literally conveying the structure of time. If taken literally, they incoherently combine the A-Theory and B-Theory of time, among other problems. Rather, I view such models as useful heuristic devices for displaying possible pasts, presents, and futures.

Objection (1) and Its Refutation

Imagining consecutive temporal moments t_n, t_{n+1}, and t_{n+2}, Malpass envisions that he is confronted with the choice at t_n of whether to flip a coin.[4] At t_{n+1}, Malpass does not flip the coin, such that the actual world is a "no-flip" world. But supposing that Malpass had flipped the coin at t_{n+1}, the coin would have landed heads or tails at t_{n+2}, which is the present moment. Malpass illustrates this situation with a branching time model, which I redraw with slight modification in Figure 3.[5]

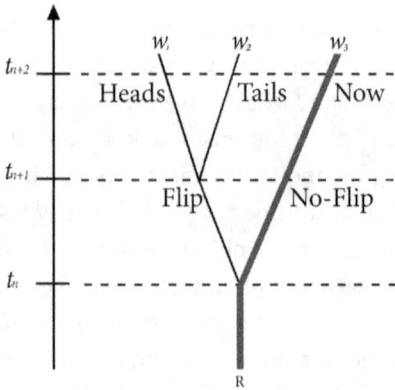

Figure 3

---

4. Malpass, "Grounding Objection," 24:30–45, labels these moments t_0, t_1, and t_2.
5. Malpass, "Grounding Objection," 24:30–45, includes the cited information and the original image.

The Logical Consistency of Molinism on Branching Time Models

The actual world, w_3, is indicated by the "thin red line" (R), while the possible world where the coin lands heads is w_1 and the possible world where the coin lands tails is w_2.[6]

Suppose that now we wish to utter the statement, "If Malpass flipped the coin at t_{n+1}, then it would land heads at t_{n+2}." Is this statement true or false? According to the Stalnaker-Lewis semantics for analyzing counterfactuals, the answer depends on whether w_1 or w_2 is closer to w_3. But the problem is that w_1 and w_2 are equally close to w_3, such that there is no non-arbitrary way to decide in w_3 whether the statement is true or false.[7] We can only give the trivial answers that if w_1 were the actual world, then the coin would land heads, and if w_2 were the actual world, then the coin would land tails. These answers are trivial because they over-specify their antecedents. For w_1 includes the coin's landing heads, and w_2 includes the coin's landing tails. So saying "if w_1 were the actual world, then the coin would land heads" is equivalent to saying "if a possible world where the coin lands heads were the actual world, then the coin would land heads," and saying "if w_2 were the actual world, then the coin would land tails" is equivalent to saying "if a possible world where the coin lands tails were the actual world, then the coin would land tails." Obviously this represents no advance in understanding! Hence Malpass concludes that there can be no truth value to our original statement, from which it follows that there can be no truth value to any counterfactual of indeterminacy. Only counterfactuals of determinacy, such as "If I would release the rock I'm holding five feet in the air, then it would fall," are true, since a possible world where the rock falls is closer to the actual world than a possible world where the rock does not fall.[8]

Immediately it could be objected that Malpass's conclusion is too hasty, reaching an ontological conclusion from epistemological evidence.[9] It is often unappreciated that the Stalnaker-Lewis semantics provide only an epistemological device—and one containing several flaws—through which humans can sometimes know the truth values of counterfactuals of determinacy. They should not be interpreted as adjudicating whether, in fact, counterfactuals of indeterminacy possess truth values. As Alvin Plantinga puts it, "We can't say that the truth of $A \to C$ is *explained* by the

---

6. Malpass, "Grounding Objection," 24:30–45.
7. Malpass, "Grounding Objection," 24:30—27:07.
8. Malpass, "Grounding Objection," 27:08—36:46.
9. Kvanvig, *All-Knowing God*, 132; Wierenga, *Nature of God*, 135.

relevant statement about possible worlds, or that the relevant similarity relation is what *makes* it true."[10] In short, Malpass has merely illustrated the epistemological point that we humans have no means of knowing the truth values of counterfactuals of indeterminacy, not the ontological point that counterfactuals of indeterminacy in fact possess no truth values. At this juncture Malpass would reply that what makes indeterminate statements true or false is the passage of time, which forces indeterminate events to either occur or not occur.[11] So time itself compelled Malpass at t_n to choose not to flip the coin at t_{n+1}. Since time only passes in the actual world, there is, contrary to the above chart's appearance, no t_{n+1} or t_{n+2} in w_1 or w_2. Without anything to make counterfactuals of indeterminacy true or false, Malpass asserts that they cannot possess truth values.[12]

Here Malpass makes an unjustified metaphysical assumption about time, whether conceived absolutely or relationally. Suppose that the correct view is absolute time, according to which time, in William Lane Craig's words, "is a duration which exists wholly independently of any events."[13] On this view, time has no causal power over events. For a cause of some event, as logician Richard Epstein points out, is roughly equivalent to a necessary and sufficient condition for that event.[14] But time cannot be necessary for some event because of its independence of that event. Even if there were no absolute time, events could still take place timelessly. Katherin Rogers correctly argues that mental events possessing a logical sequence occur in the life of God even if God experiences no duration.[15] The independence of time from events also disqualifies time from being sufficient for events. Using Malpass's example, it is Malpass acting as a free agent who decided at t_n whether to flip the coin at t_{n+1}. And if Malpass had flipped the coin at t_{n+1}, then the force at which he flipped the coin would determine its ever-changing positions, including the position when it landed. To give Malpass the benefit of the doubt here, he probably chose the coin flip to indicate an indeterminate event. So let us posit a special coin which, when flipped, is like a random number generator which will output one of two values. In short, the coin's landing position is in no way affected by how the

---

10. Plantinga, "Reply to Adams," 378.
11. Malpass, "Grounding Objection," 50:27–51:18.
12. Malpass, "Grounding Objection," 25:56–26:15.
13. Craig, "Time and the Kalam."
14. Epstein and Rooney, *Critical Thinking*, 318.
15. Rogers, "Eternity," 11–12.

flipper flipped it. But then the indeterminacy of which way the coin lands means that the landing position cannot be determined by t_{n+2}. Instead of a cause of events, absolute time is, so to speak, a recorder of which physical events happen at which physical moments. Or, more precisely, it is a frame of reference correlative with physical events according to which they can be arranged and measured.

Now suppose that the correct view of time is relational. On this view, there is a causal relationship pertaining to time and events, and Malpass has reversed the causal arrow. As Craig notes, relational time entails that "temporal relations arise as a result of the occurrence of events."[16] So events cause time, not the other way around. Assuming *arguendo* that there were no other events occurring inside or outside the universe, Malpass's choice whether to flip the coin would bring t_n into being, and in the actual world t_{n+1} and t_{n+2} would not exist. Had Malpass chosen to flip the coin, t_{n+1} would come into being upon his carrying out that choice. And t_{n+2} would come into being upon the coin's landing. Accordingly, on no view of time is Malpass correct that time causes the truth values of indeterminate statements.

We shall now proceed to demonstrate, contra Malpass, that counterfactuals of indeterminacy possess truth values. Take the pair of counterfactuals "If Malpass were to flip the special coin at t_{n+1}, then the coin would land heads at t_{n+2}." and "If Malpass were to flip the special coin at t_{n+1}, then the coin would not land heads (i.e., would land tails) at t_{n+2}." Although perhaps not universally applicable, the principle of Conditional Excluded Middle (i.e., the propositions "if such-and-such were the case, then such-and-such would be the case" and "if such-and-such were the case, then such-and-such would not be the case" are contradictories, such that exactly one is true and the other false) does apply to the "would" and "would not" statements above. For since the antecedents are sufficiently well-formed (implying the entire history of the relevant possible world up to the moment of the flip) and are directly related to their consequents (the landing of the coin), one of them must be true. Though it is not necessary *which* one is true, it is necessary *that* one of them is true in the possible world-type indicated by my dotted blue line (B) in Figure 4.[17]

---

16. Craig, "Time and the Kalam."

17. Craig, "Truth-Makers," 338. Figure 4 is an alteration of Figure 3, which is a redrawing with slight modification of the image in Malpass, "Grounding Objection," 24:30—24:45.

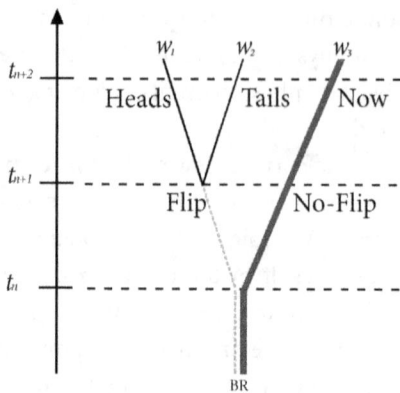

Figure 4

As Figure 4 reveals, the coin must land heads or tails at t_{n+2} if the thin blue line represented the actual history of the world up to and including t_{n+1}, such that there is no third alternative. Hence the Molinist claims there is a fact of the matter revealed by the disquotation principle. This fact could be identified as the truthmaker for one of the two counterfactuals and the false-maker, if you like, for the other counterfactual.[18]

Perhaps Malpass might now complain that there would be no way for God to know the relevant truthmaker/false-maker.[19] Though lacking the terminology, Molina would have classified this fact as an abstract object. As a divine conceptualist, Molina identified this fact, as well as all other abstract objects, as objects of God's mind. Knowledge of this fact would simply be a matter of God's knowledge by acquaintance of God's own mind.[20] To quote Molina, "God does not get His knowledge from things, but knows all things *in* Himself and *from* Himself. . . . For prior to any existence on the part of the objects, God has within Himself the means whereby He knows all things fully and perfectly."[21] Contemporary Molinists have offered other solutions. For instance, Craig proposes "that God,

18. Craig, "Truth-Makers," 346–47.

19. Malpass complains that we could not know the relevant truthmaker/false-maker in "Grounding Objection," 1:14:44—1:20:05.

20. MacGregor, *Molina*, 100–101.

21. Molina, *Foreknowledge*, 120 (4.49.12).

The Logical Consistency of Molinism on Branching Time Models

being omniscient, simply discerns all the truths there are . . . and therefore God possesses not only natural knowledge but middle knowledge as well."[22] In chapter 3, I argue that God's intuited belief about the situation just is the relevant truthmaker/false-maker. Suppose Malpass found all such explanations unconvincing. We could then reply that omniscience, defined as the property of knowing all truths and believing no falsehoods, is an essential attribute of God.[23] Even if we could not imagine *how* God could know the truth-values of counterfactuals of indeterminacy, omniscience still guarantees *that* God knows these truth-values, such that there exists a way for God to know them that lies beyond our ken. As Rogers reminds us, "reason is a less limiting faculty than imagination and may sometimes lead us to accept *that* something is true even if we cannot envision *how* it may be true."[24]

Objection 2 and Its Refutation

Malpass points out that logicians working on Molinism in the 1970s attempted to solve his first objection by positing that each node on the chart possesses its own actual future. Hence there would not merely be one thin red line but numerous thin red lines proceeding from each node.[25] Supposing *arguendo* that if Malpass flipped the coin, then it would land heads, Malpass pictures the resulting scenario with an image that I redraw with slight modification in Figure 5.[26]

Malpass then considers the tautology uttered now, "If P, then it was going to be that P." Letting P be "Malpass flipped the coin," we have the statement "If Malpass flipped the coin, then it was going to be that Malpass flipped the coin." However, Malpass claims that this tautology is now rendered false, which is absurd. For at t_{n+1} Malpass flipped the coin, but at t_n it was not going to be that Malpass flipped the coin. By *reductio*, Malpass concludes that Molinism is logically impossible. Because of this problem and

---

22. Craig, "Middle-Knowledge View," 133.
23. Craig, "Middle-Knowledge View," 137–38.
24. Rogers, "Eternity," 7.
25. Malpass, "Grounding Objection," 15:36—16:43; 36:51—38:14. The logicians to which Malpass is referring are Vaughn R. McKim and Charles C. Davis; the attempted solution is found in their "Temporal Modalities and the Future," 233–38.
26. Malpass, "Grounding Objection," 38:52—40:26, includes the cited information and the original image.

subsequent failed attempts to solve it, Malpass insinuates that philosophers of logic either have given up or should give up on Molinism.[27]

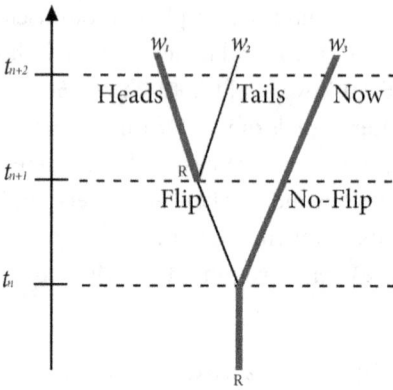

Figure 5

In response, let us first deal with Malpass's attempted *reductio*. It seems to confuse apples with oranges. All it shows is that possible pasts (and futures) ought not be treated in the same way as the actual past (and future). For on Molinism, the statement "Malpass flipped the coin" implicitly includes everything in the history of the world in which this occurred (call this background information C) up to the moment of the flip.[28] When P is fully written out as "Malpass flipped the coin in C," the tautology holds now that "If Malpass flipped the coin in C, then it was going to be that Malpass flipped the coin in C." Since C includes Malpass choosing to flip the coin at t_n, it indeed was going to be (at t_n) that Malpass flipped the coin in a world in which he chose to flip the coin at t_n.

Hence Molinism contends that in his middle knowledge God knows, for each node in the tree, its feasible (not actual) future. Borrowing but using in a different way than him Thomas Flint's terminology, the whole tree represents a "possible galaxy."[29] By "possible galaxy" I mean a cluster of possible worlds emerging from a common starting point. Working from bottom to top, the thin red line denotes the overall feasible future emerging

27. Malpass, "Grounding Objection," 38:49—40:23.
28. Craig, "Truth-Makers," 338.
29. Flint, *Divine Providence*, 51–52.

The Logical Consistency of Molinism on Branching Time Models

from the galaxy. At this moment it is not yet the actual future. However, at each node not connected to the thin red line, God knows the feasible future emerging if that node were actual, represented by some other color. This knowledge conceptually brings into being a backtracking possible history denoted by a dotted line of the same color, namely, what history would have led up to that feasible future. If the coin indeed were to land heads at t_{n+2}, the chart, correctly drawn, would feature two colors, say, red (R) and blue (B). Solid lines represent feasible segments, while dotted lines represent possible but not feasible segments. Possibility denotes logical possibility *simpliciter*, while feasibility denotes logical possibility given the facts that serve as the truthmakers of counterfactuals of indeterminacy. As Figure 6 illustrates, Molinism's insistence that tensed statements assume the past history of the possible world in which they occurred (namely, the history possessing the same color) prevents any failure of tautologies about possible worlds containing compound tenses.[30]

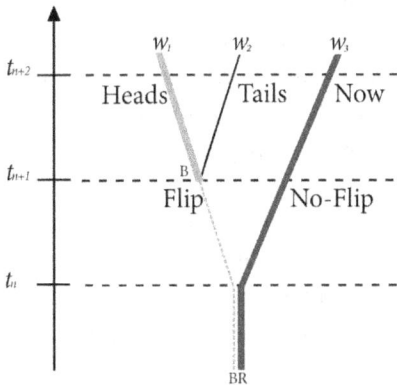

Figure 6

The thin red line only becomes the actual future when God chooses to actualize the possible galaxy pictured by the tree and thus the feasible world represented by the one continuous color (i.e., the bold line containing no dotted portions) running from bottom to top.

---

30. My solution is a variation of the solution proposed by Øhrstrøm, "Ockham and Molina," 187–88. Figure 6 is an alteration of Figure 5, which is a redrawing with slight modification of the image in Malpass, "Grounding Objection," 38:52—40:26.

Molinist Philosophical and Theological Ventures

Second, what about Malpass's insinuation that philosophical logicians either have given or should give up on Molinism? Let us begin by pointing out that even if Malpass's attempted *reductio* were sound, that does not mean that Molinism is logically impossible. It could rather mean that branching time is logically impossible. In fact, Greg Restall, who agrees with Malpass's *reductio*, concludes not that philosophical logicians should give up Molinism but that logicians inclined toward Molinism should give up branching time.[31] In fact, several prominent philosophical logicians embrace Molinism, including Torben Braüner, Per Hasle, Peter Øhrstrøm, Richard Thomason, and Anil Gupta.[32] Interestingly, Malpass admits this point while, with his co-author Jacek Wawer, insisting regarding the modal conception of "would" that characterizes Molinism: "Take it from us, this theory is killed off completely by our complaints. The interested reader can consult the gruesome details of its death."[33] However, these "gruesome details" turn out in my judgment to be merely (they say "mostly") "counter-intuitive interaction between the connectives of our language under the proposed semantics."[34] Such constitutes no actual logical failure of Molinism but merely calls into question Malpass and Wawer's language and semantics. In short, Molinism only fails if one adopts Malpass's presuppositions, which Braüner, Hasle, and Øhrstrøm do not share. This situation recalls the comment of Nuel Belnap: "If you wish to learn the 'metaphysical basis of logic' according to some logician, studying the inductive account of the language is useful, but it is crucial to understand his or her explanations of the parameters that are at bottom of the entire enterprise."[35] Malpass and Wawer simply use different parameters than Braüner, Hasle, and Øhrstrøm, and the Molinist would be inclined to embrace the latter.

---

31. Restall, "Molinism and the Thin Red Line," 235–37.

32. Braüner et al., "Determinism," 185–206; Øhrstrøm, "Ockham and Molina," 175–90; Thomason and Gupta, "Theory of Conditionals," 65–90.

33. Malpass, "Grounding Objection," 17:02–24; Malpass and Wawer, "Future for the Thin Red Line," 128, 130.

34. Malpass and Wawer, "Future for the Thin Red Line," 130. The "complaints" or "gruesome details" are found in Malpass and Wawer, "Future for the Thin Red Line," 139–40.

35. Belnap, "Indeterminist View," 97, as quoted in Øhrstrøm, "Ockham and Molina," 189.

Objection 3 and Its Refutation

Malpass complains that if each node in the chart possesses its own actual future, this forces us into the metaphysical absurdity of postulating two different types of actuality. To illustrate, Malpass informs us that he has no sister. But what sense would it make to say that if Malpass had a sister, then she would "actually choose ice cream rather than toast"? How can a hypothetical sister actually do anything?[36] To begin with, no Molinist would endorse the assertion that if Malpass had a hypothetical sister, then she would actually choose ice cream rather than toast. The Molinist could only posit that if Malpass had an actual sister (or actually had a sister), then she would actually choose ice cream rather than toast, so avoiding the equivocation problem entirely. But more importantly, the Molinist denies that each node in the chart possesses an actual future. Hence the mistake lies with the logicians in the 1970s who failed to differentiate various feasible futures in a possible galaxy with different colors and, if not branching off from the feasible past, linking them to possible but not feasible backtracking pasts of the same colors.

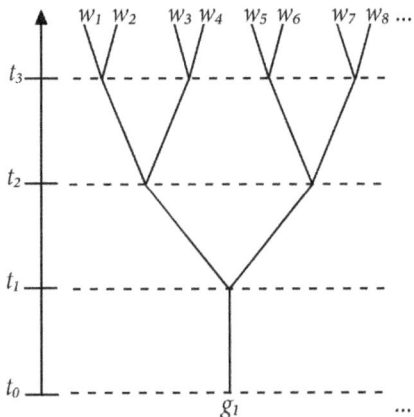

Figure 7

---

36. Malpass, "Grounding Objection," 40:40—41:22.

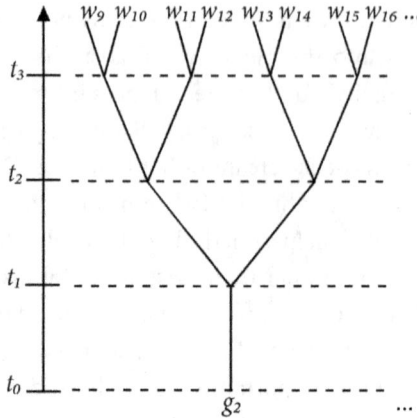

Figure 8

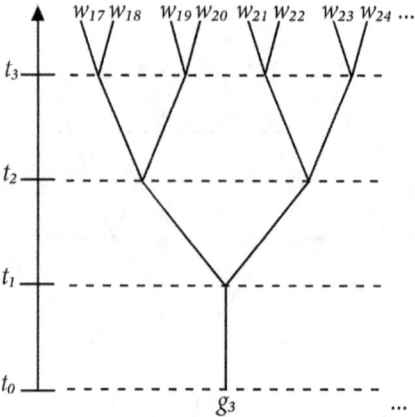

Figure 9

Indeed branching time models help us to illuminate the first and second logical moments of divine omniscience. In the first moment, God's natural knowledge, God knows all possible galaxies, represented by g_1, g_2, g_3, ..., and thus all possible worlds, represented by w_1–w_{24}. ... Each galaxy contains unique starting conditions at t_0 and so unique events at t_1, t_2, and

The Logical Consistency of Molinism on Branching Time Models

t_3. In other words, any indeterminate events at each time are different in each galaxy. This is shown in Figure 7, Figure 8, and Figure 9.

Since God only knows at this moment what *could* be, there are no colored lines yet.

In the second moment, God's middle knowledge, God knows the feasible futures emerging from any node (t_1, t_2, t_3) in every possible galaxy. The thin red line in each galaxy is that galaxy's only continuous line (i.e., the line featuring no dotted portion) from bottom to top. The other non-black colors (blue (B), green (G), yellow (Y)) are solid only from the node at which their feasible future begins (t_2 or t_3). At that node they backtrack as dotted lines to the trunk of their tree. As represented by each thin red line, God knows the one feasible world emerging from each possible galaxy. Any non-continuous line (i.e., a line that features at least one dotted portion) is known by God to be a merely possible but not feasible world. To put the last two sentences another way, a feasible world consists of all feasible futures from bottom to top, while a merely possible world does not consist of all feasible futures from bottom to top. This is shown in Figure 10, Figure 11, and Figure 12.

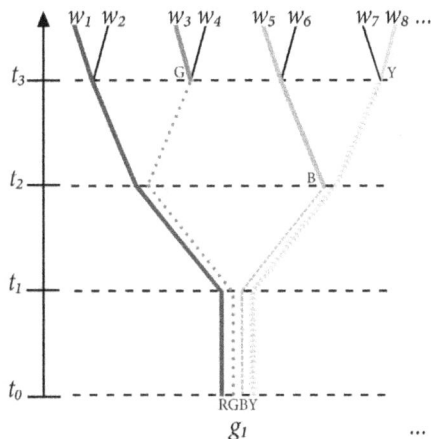

Figure 10

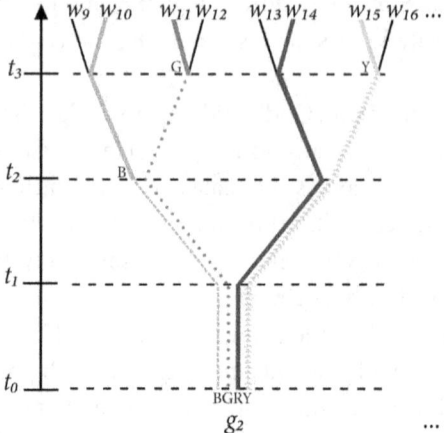

Figure 11

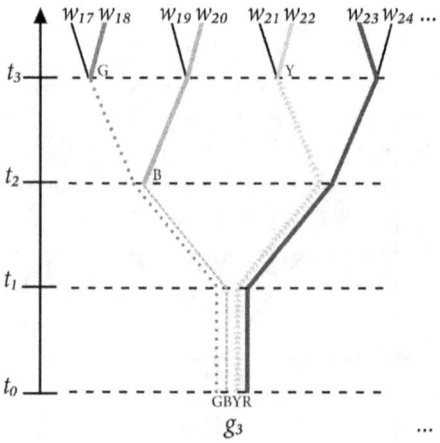

Figure 12

From the three possible galaxies, we see that w_1, w_{14}, and w_{23} are the only three feasible worlds, while w_2–w_{13}, w_{15}–w_{22}, and w_{24} are merely possible worlds. Let us suppose that, in God's creative decision, God chooses to actualize w_{23}. This feasible world now becomes the actual world, and the thin red line in g_3 becomes the actual future. From the actual world, we can consider the other possible worlds within our galaxy and thereby make true

The Logical Consistency of Molinism on Branching Time Models

counterfactual statements about them, such as what would have happened if Malpass flipped the coin or had a sister.

These insights put us in a position to illustrate how a literal reading of Matthew 11:20–24 proves consistent with transworld damnation. Aaron Fitzwater proposes that the repentance of the inhabitants of Tyre and Sidon and the repentance of the inhabitants of Sodom are feasible futures belonging to merely possible, not feasible, worlds. The CCFs describing these acts of repentance are not compossible with any full set of chronologically prior CCFs. In other words, the worlds in which these events occur do not consist of all feasible futures from bottom to top. Hence the CCFs narrated in Matthew 11:20–24 possess antecedents whose falsity is factually (not logically) necessary.[37]

Regarding these worlds, we know the repentance of the relevant agents is feasible. Since counterfactuals of divine freedom are the result of God's creative decision, Jesus' free decision to perform miracles at first-century CE Tyre and Sidon or at nineteenth-century BCE Sodom constitutes a feasible future. However, given the chronologically prior CCFs, something preceding Jesus' decision to do either is not feasible, making factually necessary the falsity of his doing either. Looking at w_{20}, for example, Jesus' free decision to perform the miracles would represent the solid blue line at t_2 and the repentance of the relevant agents would represent the continuation of the solid blue line at t_3, while something leading up to the solid blue line is dotted blue. Perhaps in any world where Jesus traveled openly enough in Tyre or Sidon to perform the numerous public miracles actually done in Chorazin and Bethsaida (see Mark 7:24), Roman officials would have assassinated him before he could have performed them. Likewise, perhaps in any world where the Incarnation occurred in nineteenth-century BCE Canaan, Jesus would have been murdered by the wicked inhabitants of Sodom before he could have performed there the numerous public miracles actually done in Capernaum. Accordingly, there is no feasible world in which the inhabitants of Tyre, Sidon, or Sodom who are in fact lost would have been saved, so rendering these persons transworld damned.

Conclusion

My proposals that, for any possible galaxy, (a) there is only one thin red line, (b) any feasible future at any node not connected to the thin red line

---

37. Personal correspondence with Fitzwater.

conceptually generates a backtracking possible but not feasible history, and (c) conditional statements containing compound tenses need to be evaluated from the perspective of the possible or feasible history that they presuppose, defeat Malpass's three purported logical objections to Molinism. Moreover, these three proposals render Molinism logically consistent on branching time models, which in turn help to illuminate the distinctions between possibility, feasibility, and actuality.

— 7 —

Molinism, Apologetics, and Music

THIS CHAPTER ENDEAVORS TO construct a philosophically and theologically plausible account of how music becomes holy or numinous and the epistemological role holy music plays. It then shows how this account is harmonious with the reflections of various prominent theologians from the second century through today. In a similar fashion to Rudolf Otto (1869–1937), I conceive of holiness or numinousness as the state of being suffused with the presence of God and efficaciously mediating the divine to one or more persons.[1] Whether sacred or secular, all music is potentially holy or non-holy, and no music is intrinsically holy or non-holy. That is to say, any musical piece or performance has the ability to embody and bring a person into relationship with God, and no musical piece or performance does this for all persons in all places at all times. My primary conversation partners in developing my account are, in chronological order, Luis de Molina, Karl Barth, and Alvin Plantinga.

Theological Prolegomena

We start by proposing, with Molina, that an ineradicable part of the *imago Dei* in which humans were created is what philosophers call libertarian free will, or the will's ability to choose between various alternatives in all matters that fall under its purview. Although involuntary matters (e.g., my heart

1. Otto, *Holy*, 5–40.

beating, my digestive system working) do not fall under the will's purview, libertarian free will guarantees that I can choose, say, to play my trumpet or to not play my trumpet, and for whatever alternative I choose, I could have chosen otherwise. Molina insisted that also falling under the will's purview is the ability to positively or negatively respond to God.[2]

We delve deeper into anthropology by availing ourselves of the A/C (Aquinas/Calvin) model of Plantinga.[3] According to the A/C model, one of the many cognitive faculties humans possess is the *sensus divinitatis* (sense of the divine), which, when properly functioning, automatically outputs various beliefs about God.[4] The concept of the *sensus divinitatis* was first proposed by John Calvin.[5] Beliefs produced by the *sensus divinitatis* are properly basic, arising appropriately from our experience but may or may not be able to be proved by our experience. However, in the absence of any defeaters (disproofs), we are rational to believe them.[6] However, we are not compelled to believe them, as properly basic beliefs are resistible by the will. For Plantinga, a cognitive faculty is properly functioning if it is functioning in circumstances in which it is designed to operate.[7] Thus proper function may be adversely affected by a number of psychological and moral factors, such as personal history, maturity level, personal taste, and engagement with sin. To illustrate, someone forced to go camping who hates the outdoors may see a beautiful starry night and feel absolutely nothing religious, since the person's hatred of the outdoors constitute circumstances in which the *sensus divinitatis* is not designed to function. However, if that person loved or was even neutral to the outdoors, the *sensus divinitatis* may have been triggered by the starlit scene to output belief that God created the universe or that God is supremely majestic.

Barth famously, or perhaps infamously, claimed that the Bible is not intrinsically the Word of God—a status which exclusively belongs to Jesus

---

2. MacGregor, *Molina*, 75.

3. In *Warranted Christian Belief*, Plantinga offers both the A/C model (168–98) and the extended A/C model (241–89), the latter of which presupposes the Reformed doctrines of total depravity and total inability. Because these doctrines are incompatible with Molina's insistence on libertarian free will, I will restrict myself to using only the A/C model, which stipulates no inherent cognitive impairment.

4. Plantinga, *Warranted Christian Belief*, 172.

5. Calvin, *Institutes* 1.3.1.

6. Plantinga, *Warranted Christian Belief*, 177–78. I have heard William Lane Craig describe properly basic beliefs this way on several occasions.

7. Plantinga, *Warranted Christian Belief*, 110–13.

Christ—but is rather a witness to the Word of God.[8] Barth held that the Bible contained numerous errors and contradictions, extending even to the theological level. Despite these inherent defects, Barth maintained that the Bible becomes the Word of God when God chooses to use it to effect someone's personal encounter with God's own self.[9] While disagreeing with Barth's view of the Bible, I propose that what Barth incorrectly says of the Bible can be correctly applied to music. Having laid the necessary groundwork, we launch into our exploration of music.

How Music Becomes Holy

In Barthian fashion, I maintain that music, whether sacred or secular, possesses many theological errors on account of the fallible humans who compose and perform it. Such errors are not limited to lyrical music but also extend to purely tonal music, in which God or part of God's creation is depicted in a theologically incorrect mood. Nonetheless, music becomes holy when God chooses to imbue it with God's presence and effectuate someone's personal encounter with God. If a thinker subscribes to theological determinism (i.e., a hard determinism in which God causes all things irrespective of human wills) or theological compatibilism (i.e., a soft determinism in which God causes all things even while humans always act on their greatest desires), then the account could end here. But if humans have libertarian free will, then God's choosing to suffuse a musical piece or performance with God's presence is not sufficient to ensure that the music will efficaciously communicate God's presence to someone. There are two additional factors, the second of which depends entirely on the intended human target of communication.

First, the target's *sensus divinitatis* must be properly functioning—with all the complexity that proper function involves—to output relevant theistic beliefs upon seeing or hearing the music. It seems that an omnipotent God could guarantee, supernaturally if necessary, that any person's *sensus divinitatis* properly functions at some point. Second, the target must freely accept these beliefs and properly respond to them by opening oneself to God's personal revelation in the music. Even an omnipotent being cannot guarantee this, as it is logically impossible to make someone freely do something. Indeed, it is quite doubtful that God would engage in the

8. Barth, *Church Dogmatics*, 1/1:436; 1/1:111–16.
9. Barth, *Church Dogmatics*, 1/1:109–10.

Molinist Philosophical and Theological Ventures

pointless exercise of suffusing God's own presence in music if God knew that it would accomplish nothing—namely, that no one, either performer or hearer, would enter into relationship with God! The question arising at this juncture is: can God know such a thing?

In response to this, we apprise ourselves of Molina's doctrine of middle knowledge, namely, God's prevolitional knowledge of all true hypothetical conditionals (i.e., if such-and-such were the case, so-and-so would be the case). By virtue of God's middle knowledge, God knows, for any possible libertarian free (hereafter, free) person God could create, what their relevant musical factors, such as musical background, education, abilities, tastes, listening habits, receptivity levels, and so forth, would be under any conceivable set of circumstances. God also knows, for any possible free person God could create, what their relevant non-musical factors, such as psychological dispositions, family relationships, friendships, loves, hates, righteous decisions, sinful decisions, and so forth, would be under any conceivable set of circumstances. In view of all this, God knows for every possible free individual how their *sensus divinitatis* would function and how they would freely respond to the *sensus divinitatis* if God were to imbue music with God's own presence. Since this knowledge is prevolitional, God apprehends it, logically speaking, before God makes the decision to create any world, much less a world of free creatures.[10]

According to Molina, God uses this knowledge to providentially craft the world God will create. In God's "absolutely complete and unlimited deliberation," God plans the world down to the last detail, not by precluding or overpowering human free decisions, but by working both through and in spite of human free decisions.[11] In particular, God can construct a world in which all persons at some point find themselves in encounters with music where, if God were to reveal God's own self through it, the *sensus divinitatis* would function properly and so automatically present to the will the opportunity to directly experience God in the music. If God middle-knows that some but not necessarily all performers or hearers would respond by entering into communion with God, God suffuses the music with God's presence and so makes it holy. God's musical presence is extrinsically efficacious in bringing persons into relationship with God, as it does not do this for everyone automatically but does this only for those who would freely respond appropriately.

10. Molina, *Foreknowledge*, 170 (4.52.10).
11. Molina, *Foreknowledge*, 173 (4.52.13); Craig, "Middle-Knowledge View," 122.

Molinism, Apologetics, and Music

As a result, some persons will encounter that same holy music—made ontologically distinct from non-holy music by virtue of the divine presence—and, for one reason or another, do not enter that presence. For certain of these persons, their *sensus divinitatis* functions improperly based on the musical and non-musical factors sketched above. For others of these persons, their *sensus divinitatis* does function properly—outputting the belief that God is immediately present in the music to be experienced—but they freely resist the invitation. This account explains why various persons react differently to holy music. For example, on August 6, 2019, I heard Lauren Daigle's song "You Say" on the radio and—assuming the reliability of my judgment—entered into the divine presence. On this account, God imbued that particular playing of "You Say" with God's presence, thus making it holy music. Someone else listening to the song may not like contemporary Christian music (such as my mother), may not agree with the view of justification proffered by the song (such as some of my theological colleagues), may not be paying attention to the song (such as my young son), or any of a myriad other reasons that would cause their *sensus divinitatis* to malfunction. And someone else listening to the song might correctly sense God present in the music but willingly resist this self-presenting belief based on one's preference for atheism or one's view of oneself as self-reliant and autonomous, not needing divine approval, and so fail to enter into musical fellowship with God.

Does this account require that every person, at some point in their life, performs or hears holy music? It seems not, though probably most people do. Now the account does presuppose that God has constructed a world where each person at least once in their life encounters music and, were God to imbue it with God's presence, their *sensus divinitatis* would properly function. God can guarantee this much through omnipotence. But there are likely some persons who would never freely respond appropriately to holy music if their *sensus divinitatis* were to properly function. Omnipotence cannot eliminate this prospect. For such persons, God is under no obligation to make sure that their life includes the experience of holy music. We may posit that God would not engage in the fruitless task of imbuing music with God's presence for their sake.

So for any person who would freely avail oneself of the opportunity, God gives the opportunity to directly encounter God through music. The only persons whom God withholds this opportunity are persons whom God middle-knows would under no circumstances freely enter God's presence upon experiencing holy music. Thus no one who fails to experience holy music could say, "God, it's unfair that I never encountered you through holy music." For God would respond, "No, it's perfectly fair, because I middle-knew that even if you had experienced holy music and your *sensus divinitatis* had properly functioned, you would have freely resisted me."[12]

The Epistemological Role of Holy Music

Now we come to a different question—what epistemic status does a person's belief, generated by the *sensus divinitatis*, that God is revealing God's own self through the music—a belief which presupposes theistic belief in general—have? Does the person genuinely know through music that God exists and that they have encountered God? Or do they merely believe, albeit truly, these things? To illustrate the difference, epistemologists, or theorists of knowledge, emphasize that true belief alone does not equal knowledge.[13] Suppose I lack perfect pitch and hear Beethoven's *Emperor Concerto*, lacking any information about the key of the music. But suppose I believe that the piece is in concert E♭ Major, thus just happening to be correct. In this case, I have true belief about the concerto's key but obviously do not know the concerto's key. By contrast, someone with perfect pitch would know—assuming the person is not mentally impaired—the piece is in concert E♭ Major. The difference between the two cases, per Plantinga, is warrant. For him, knowledge is warranted true belief. Warrant means the state of a belief's being produced by a properly functioning cognitive faculty.[14] Perfect pitch is a mental faculty which, when properly functioning, yields accurate beliefs about musical notes and therefore keys.

Regarding the belief produced by the *sensus divinitatis*, the *sensus divinitatis* of the person is functioning properly and yields the beliefs in theism and direct personal encounter with God. Hence the person in question possesses warrant for one's true belief and genuinely knows it.[15] This has the amazing implication that holy music plays an apologetic function, furnishing people with actual knowledge of God's existence and even

---

12. A similar explanation of why some but not all people receive special revelation is given by Craig, "'No Other Name,'" 183–85.
13. Pojman and Vaughn, *Philosophy*, 196.
14. Plantinga, *Warranted Christian Belief*, 153–54.
15. Plantinga, *Warranted Christian Belief*, 149.

presence. William Edgar discusses "the relationship of music to apologetics" as follows:

> Does music's aesthetic quality prove the existence of a supreme being full of glory? The ancient world thought there was such a connection. Plato argues in *Timaeus* that music, especially inaudible sounds, is given by God (through the *Muses*) in order to harmonize our souls and bring them into conformity with heavenly realities. Immanuel Kant considered "the art of tone" to be a universal language, directing our souls upwards through obedience to various objective rules.[16]

Accordingly, apologetics is no longer limited to philosophical arguments for, say, the existence of God or historical arguments for, say, the resurrection of Jesus, but music is equally important in the apologetic task. Our account therefore opens up apologetics to churches (often theologically moderate and liberal churches), groups, and individuals that are quite skeptical of traditional apologetics.

Support for the Proposed Account from Past to Present

The ontological distinction between holy and non-holy music was not lost on the Church Fathers. Although space does not permit an exhaustive list, a representative sample of quotations from the Patristic corpus will suffice to illustrate the Fathers' conviction that music which did result in personal encounter with God for anyone was not holy. An extreme example comes from Clement of Alexandria (c. 150–215). In his *Pædagogus* (c. 200), Clement of Alexandria appealed to the divergent results of non-holy and holy music to draw a sharp contrast between the two types. For him, non-holy music results in people becoming "quite immodest and intractable" and among "the superstitious who are engrossed in idolatry." Non-holy music yields "every improper sight and sound, to speak in a word, and every shameful sensation of licentiousness—which, in truth, is privation of sensation." But "the Spirit, distinguishing from such revelry the divine service, sings, 'Praise Him with the sound of trumpet'; for with sound of trumpet He shall raise the dead. 'Praise Him on the psaltery'; for the tongue is the psaltery of the Lord. 'And praise Him on the lyre.' By the lyre is meant the mouth struck by the Spirit, as it were by a plectrum. . . . *In the present instance He*

---

16. Edgar, "Music," 462.

is a guest with us" (*Pædagogus* 2.4, emphasis added).[17] Here we observe that the Holy Spirit, who is the very presence of God, produces holy music, using human tongues and mouths as instruments, and becomes our guest in its performance.

In line with Platonism, Clement's *Protrepticus* (c. 202) asserted that Christ was the prototypical or ideal "New Song" who imbues holy music with its numinous dimension (*Protrepticus* 1). Just as Christ was fully present during his ministry, so every "new song" makes Christ fully present. In contrast to "old songs," which enslave people to the present evil age, the "new songs" Clement championed free people from their spiritual bondage and bring them into saving relationship with God. Any new song "has come to loose, and that speedily, the bitter bondage of tyrannizing demons; and leading us back to the mild and loving yoke of piety, recalls to heaven those that had been cast prostrate to the earth" (*Protrepticus* 1).[18] Clement's ontological conception of holy music was filled with epistemological substance by Basil of Caesarea (330–379). In his homily on Psalm 1, Basil asserts that the Holy Spirit gave humanity holy music so that, "while in appearance they sing, [they] may in reality be educating their souls."[19] Since education is, by definition, the transmission of knowledge, holy music furnishes persons with knowledge.

Shifting to the medieval period, Aquinas (1225–1274) formulated a hierarchy of the arts headed by Christ, the one fully encompassing art of God. While not addressing music in particular, Aquinas argued that fine arts in general have as their goal to foster relational union with God the Trinity; hence the ontological quality of any artistic endeavor is directly proportional to how well it performs this goal.[20] Applying Aquinas' theory of the arts to music, holy music mediates the beauty, goodness, and truth of God to its hearers. Holy music possesses the capacity to convey the power and being of God. By contrast, non-holy music fails to convey something of the divine essence. It manipulates the flesh instead of engaging the spirit, and it substitutes the impotent acquaintance between an "I" and some particular "It" for the beholder's personally transformative relationship with the universal Thou.[21]

17. Translated by Coxe, *Ante-Nicene Fathers*, 2:248–49.
18. Translated by Coxe, *Ante-Nicene Fathers*, 2:171–72.
19. Basil of Caesarea, "Homily," 65.
20. Aquinas, *Summa Theologiae* 1.45.6; MacGregor, "Aquinas," 233.
21. MacGregor, "Aquinas," 245–46.

Molinism, Apologetics, and Music

In the Reformation era, John Calvin (1509–1564) stipulated that holy music is produced by God, and when people sing holy songs, God places its content in their mouths and unites them with God and the angels:

> What St. Augustine has said is true, that no one is able to sing things worthy of God except that which he has received from him. . . . And moreover, when we sing them, we are certain that God puts in our mouths these things, as if he himself were singing in us to exalt his glory. Wherefore Chrysostom exhorts, as well as the men, the women and the little children to accustom themselves to singing them, in order that this may be a sort of meditation to associate themselves with the company of the angels. . . . What is there now to do? It is to have songs not only honest, but also holy. (*Preface to the Genevan Psalter*)[22]

Since Calvin originated the notion of the *sensus divinitatis*, it stands to reason that he would take holy music as engendering immediate knowledge of God.

Finally, our account resonates with the work of Jeremy Begbie on faithful worship. Supposing that holy music is part of faithful worship, Begbie claims that faithful worship reorients us to God and that the Holy Spirit indwells us to accomplish this reorientation.[23] Moreover, Begbie alleges that faithful worship occurs "*with and through Christ.*"[24] Faithful worship is therefore "a sharing by the Spirit in the Son's communion with the Father by the Spirit."[25] Begbie holds that faithful worship is a truthful activity in which humans acquire knowledge "through the Spirit and with Christ."[26] In faithful worship, we are "re-directed to the Father through the Son by the Spirit" and so "discover the love that is eternally given and received between Father and Son, the love with which we can be bound together (John 17:21)."[27] Begbie goes so far as to say that in faithful worship we are "caught up in the life of the triune God."[28] In view of our supposition, holy music empowers us to participate in the intra-trinitarian being of God and is the instrument through which God imparts knowledge to us.

---

22. Translated by Garside, *Pseaumes*, 4.
23. Begbie, "Faithful Feelings," 335.
24. Begbie, "Faithful Feelings," 336.
25. Begbie, "Faithful Feelings," 337.
26. Begbie, "Faithful Feelings," 337.
27. Begbie, "Faithful Feelings," 337.
28. Begbie, "Faithful Feelings," 337.

Conclusion

Bringing Molina, Barth, and Plantinga into conversation, this chapter has furnished an account that music is not intrinsically holy but becomes holy when God chooses to imbue it with God's presence in order to effectuate a personal encounter with at least one other individual. God decides when to do this on the basis of God's middle knowledge. In cases where God middle-knows that if God were to imbue music with the divine presence, then the *sensus divinitatis* of at least one performer or hearer would function properly and at least one of these same performers or hearers would freely respond to the output of the *sensus divinitatis* by entering into relationship with God, God suffuses music with God's presence and makes it holy. This has the consequence that holy music is more common than is often surmised.

When many people encounter holy music, either their *sensus divinitatis* does not function properly for various reasons or they freely choose to resist the drawings to God afforded by the *sensus divinitatis*. However, it may be the case that some persons never perform or hear holy music, such that none of the music they encounter in their lives is imbued with God's own presence. Via God's middle knowledge, God ensures that the only persons in world history who never encounter holy music are persons who, if they were to encounter holy music, would not respond appropriately to it. But for every person who would under any circumstances enter into God's presence through holy music, God providentially ensures that they in fact experience holy music when their *sensus divinitatis* is properly functioning and so enter into musical fellowship with God.

Holy music affords persons who positively respond to it with knowledge—and not mere true belief—that God exists and that they have encountered God. Thus music is a powerful apologetic and, in my judgment, ought to be appropriated as such. While this account has, to my knowledge, no previous anticipation, it is consistent with the reflections of several past and present luminaries in the Christian tradition.

— 8 —

The Relationship between Molinism and Eventual Universalism

ON THE PUBLIC TELEVISION show *Closer to Truth*, Molinist philosopher Alvin Plantinga discussed what I call eventual universalism, namely, the view that hell exists and that the reprobate go to hell but eventually learn from the error of their ways and turn to God, whereupon God ultimately gives them eternal life. Without affirming that the Bible teaches eventual universalism, Plantinga states that several biblical texts suggest universalism, citing 1 Corinthians 15:22 ("as all die in Adam, so all will be made alive in Christ") as an example. From this and similar texts Plantinga muses, "Maybe people get second chances, third chances after death, fourth chances, nth chances. . . . And maybe it will be that in the long run nobody finally turns God down. Everybody finally says okay." Plantinga concludes his discussion of eventual universalism by remarking, "I don't myself quite believe it but I don't disbelieve it either. I think it's something that a Christian should at least hope for."[1] While I am a disbeliever in eventual universalism, I sympathize with Plantinga's position and would very much like to be wrong about my disbelief.

In the branch of the Anabaptist tradition to which I belong (the Church of the Brethren), eventual universalism was held by founder Alexander

---

1. Plantinga, "Can a Person Be a Soul?," 1:40—4:37.

Molinist Philosophical and Theological Ventures

Mack (1679–1735) and most other first-generation Brethren leaders.[2] The view receded by the mid-nineteenth century, due in my judgment to a continuation of Mack's fear that it would provoke earthly faithlessness and moral laxity among unbelievers.[3] While not a dominant belief among contemporary Brethren, eventual universalism is still considered in my community a live option for the individual believer. Other Christian communities containing a sizeable proportion of evangelicals are not as tolerant of eventual universalism as my own. Many evangelicals vilify eventual universalism as a dangerous heresy, fearing that the view will result in a decline of evangelism and the church's failure to complete the Great Commission.[4] Whatever if any legitimacy there is to the nineteenth-century Brethren and contemporary evangelical fears, neither logically imply that eventual universalism is false. At best they show that the doctrine could be abused for deleterious ends, comparable to the abusing of *sola fide* for such ends as antinomianism and disregard for social justice.[5]

This brings us to the question of the relationship between Molinism and universalism. Molina himself subscribed to what I dub the eternalist view, namely, that those who die in a lost state remain in hell forever, owing

---

2. Mack, *Complete Writings*, 98–99; Stoffer, *Brethren Doctrines*, 82, 112; Durnbaugh, *Fruit of the Vine*, 168–71.

3. Durnbaugh, *Fruit of the Vine*, 171–72; Mack, *Complete Writings*, 98–99.

4. For representative examples see McClymond and Copan, "Universalism"; Strange, "Universalism."

5. In fairness to eventual universalism, I believe that manifestations of these fears are in fact abuses of the doctrine. They would, however, be legitimate inferences if the brand of universalism under discussion held that there were no hell and that all people, upon death, would be admitted into heaven to share in exactly the same blessings. But any period of time in hell represents an incalculable loss to an individual, and I concur with Mack concerning the state of any once denizens of hell, "Even if at some time the torment should end after long eternities, they will never attain that which the believers have achieved in the time of grace through Jesus Christ if they obey Him" (*Writings*, 98). In other words, there would be incalculably great eternal benefits for persons who embrace and are allegiant to God during the earthly life upon which those who do not will forever miss out. To give an analogy, imagine that you, without harm to yourself, could prevent someone from getting hit by a car. Suppose you know that if they were struck, they would suffer permanent paraplegia and severe brain damage that, after thirty years of treatment, would be reversed. Would you for a moment think, "Well, there's no urgency for me to prevent the person from getting hit; after all, I know it won't be fatal"? Of course not! The analogy applies equally well to preventing yourself from getting hit by the car. To an infinitely greater degree, Christians should not lessen evangelism and unbelievers should not continue to live in sin if they think it will only lead to an incalculably great but not the greatest conceivable loss.

not to his philosophical theology but to his interpretation of Scripture. Notice that by the eternalist view I do not imply that hell entails flames but rather an eternal lack of the beatific vision. Interestingly, most contemporary Molinist philosophers use Molinism to defend the eternalist view. On the other hand, R. Zachary Manis has recently argued that Molinism strongly implies eventual universalism, and Eric Reitan maintains that the doctrine of libertarian freedom (a Molinist *sine qua non*) guarantees the truth of eventual universalism.[6] In this chapter I defend three contentions. First, Molinism renders eternalism logically possible and not necessarily improbable. Second, Molinism renders eventual universalism logically possible and not necessarily improbable. Third, if libertarian human freedom is true, then Molinism is the only way universalism can succeed. Accordingly, given Molinism, neither eternalism nor eventual universalism is ruled out. If Molinism is true, then the debate between eternalism and eventual universalism can only be settled on biblical grounds, not philosophical ones. Of course, biblical and/or philosophical considerations may be used to contest Molinism, which, if successful, would bring philosophical grounds back into play for settling the debate between eternalism and eventual universalism. Moreover, any form of universalism that embraces libertarian human freedom requires Molinism.

Molinism and Eternalism

At first glance, it seems easy to maintain that Molinism renders eternalism logically possible. If the human soul possesses libertarian freedom, as Molinism holds, then it is possible for certain souls to separate themselves from God during their earthly sojourn and to forever continue their rejection of any divine overtures to save them. Suppose God middle-knows that this possibility obtains in all feasible worlds. Then God must choose either to create a world featuring eternalism or no world at all. God proceeds to create a world, specifically, a salvifically optimal one. Yet it is precisely this scenario that has been challenged as highly problematic. Manis calls the above scenario "the *no-feasible-universalist-world hypothesis* (NFUW)."[7] He finds this view untenable largely because the reasons he can see why God would create a world therein either compromise God's omnibenevolence, are highly improbable, or both.

6. Manis, *Sinners*, 120–34; Reitan, "Guarantee of Universal Salvation," 422–30.

7. Manis, *Sinners*, 127.

Molinist Philosophical and Theological Ventures

Manis considers two versions of NFUW. We shall call the first version NFUW *simpliciter*. On this version, for every possible person P, P would freely appropriate salvation in some salvifically optimal feasible worlds, P would freely and eternally reject salvation in some salvifically optimal feasible worlds, and P would not exist in some salvifically optimal feasible worlds. If God chooses to actualize a salvifically optimal feasible world, then some people who are lost in the actual world would have been saved in an equally good feasible world. Manis seems to imply that this scenario makes God out to be an essentially unloving and unjust consequentialist, as "God has to *sacrifice* some individuals."[8] Manis also finds this scenario incredible, arguing that "the failure of Molinists to produce any plausible explanation of NFUW is thus itself a good reason to reject M-AU [i.e., Molinist anti-universalism]."[9] To his credit, Manis tries to find a plausible explanation of this scenario, one that partially anticipates my explanation.[10] Suppose that traducianism, according to which human beings reproduce body and soul, is true rather than soul-creationism, according to which human beings reproduce only bodily and, at some point, God specially creates the soul and infuses it into the conceptus. In that case, no P could have a different lineage and still be P. Suppose further that, in view of traducianism, the only sets of compossible circumstances that solidify into feasible worlds are those in which the existence of each person who would be freely saved is dependent on *the existence* of at least one person who, despite God's every effort to save them both on earth and in hell, would be eternally damned. However, neither the existence nor the salvation of anyone who would be saved is dependent on the *eternal damnation* of anyone who would be eternally damned. Moreover, God does not create anyone for the purpose of their being eternally damned. God genuinely intends for the salvation of all, giving for all eternity those who would be damned the quantity and quality of grace that would be most likely to secure their salvation, but they forever continue to reject it.

Manis's characterization of God's sacrificing some presupposes that it is better for a person not to exist than to exist and be eternally damned. This is far from obvious on my understanding of hell, which entails not receiving the beatific vision, namely, not being in the definitive presence of God. However, in hell one is spiritually separated from but still in the

---

8. Manis, *Sinners*, 132.
9. Manis, *Sinners*, 130.
10. Manis, *Sinners*, 130n33.

The Relationship between Molinism and Eventual Universalism

repletive presence of God. God's definitive presence is the qualitatively highest mode of the divine presence in heaven, while God's repletive presence is a qualitatively lesser mode of the divine presence in which God fills all locations in the universe and in hell. Being in God's repletive presence is an intrinsic good and, even if it occurs in hell, is far better for the creature than not existing at all. As the twentieth-century philosophical theologian Paul Tillich pointed out, "the threat of nonbeing," not hell, constitutes every human's greatest existential threat.[11] To this Manis could object with Jesus' words to Judas, "For the Son of Man goes as it is written of him, but woe to that one by whom the Son of Man is betrayed! It would have been better for that one not to have been born" (Mark 14:21; see also Matt 26:24). The assumption of this potential objection is that "it would have been better for that one not to have been born" means "it would have been better for that one not to exist because he would go to hell." But, on this assumption, the text entails that neither universalism nor NFUW *simpliciter* is true, rendering the potential objection a fruitless one for a universalist like Manis to actually make (and which he does not make). For the universalist holds that it is better for Judas to exist than not because the eternity Judas will spend in God's definitive presence after being released from hell outweighs even any conscious torment he will experience in hell. Thus both the universalist and the proponent of NFUW *simpliciter* must deny the key assumption, and I think this is the hermeneutically correct move to make.

For, most probably, Jesus is here employing the first-century Jewish device of metalepsis, or alluding to at least one Hebrew Bible passage "in a way that evokes resonances of the earlier text *beyond those explicitly cited*."[12] Jesus is seemingly alluding to two passages in his remark to Judas. The first is Jeremiah 20:14–18, in which Jeremiah complains:

> Cursed be the day on which I was born! The day when my mother bore me, let it not be blessed! Cursed be the man who brought the news to my father, saying, "A child is born to you, a son," making him very glad. Let that man be like the cities that the LORD overthrew without pity; let him hear a cry in the morning and an alarm at noon, because he did not kill me in the womb; so my mother would have been my grave, and her womb forever great. Why did I come forth from the womb to see toil and sorrow, and spend my days in shame?

---

11. Tillich, *Systematic Theology*, 1:208; see also 1:14. Annihilationists would disagree with my sentiment here.

12. Hays, *Conversion*, 2.

Here Jeremiah's notion of "being better for that one not to have been born" is not nonexistence but his existing and then being deliberately killed in the womb. The second passage to which Jesus seemingly refers is Job 3:16, in which Job complains, "why was I not buried like a stillborn child, like an infant that never sees the light?" Likewise, Job's notion of "being better for that one not to have been born" is not nonexistence but his existing and then naturally dying in the womb. Thus the point of Jesus' remark to Judas is that it would have been better if Judas had existed and then experienced miscarriage or abortion than if Judas was born and grew up to betray Jesus.

On my proposed explanation of NFUW and depiction of hell, then, it is worse for no world to exist than for a world to exist containing some P who are freely saved but would have been freely lost in another equally good world and other P who are freely lost but would have been freely saved in another equally good world. A world better than this is ruled out *ex hypothesi*. Accordingly, God is not unloving in choosing to create such a salvifically optimal feasible world. Moreover, the notion that God is unjust is ruled out by the Doctrine of Double Effect (DDE), according to which one's performance of the best possible action is justified if any harms eventuating from this action, though foreknown, are not intended. Clearly God does not intend the eternal damnation of anyone but does everything in his power to prevent it. Hence God's middle knowledge of the lost's eternal damnation does not render it unjust for God to create such a world. Manis rejects any DDE defense to NFUW *simpliciter* because, on his view, it unacceptably results in God's sacrifice of some, a claim I have already contested.[13] I would also point out that, on my proposal, God is not a consequentialist because he is not using anyone's damnation as a means to the end of other people's salvation. God would only be a consequentialist if the saved's beatitude depends on the damnation of others (i.e., if P_2 is only saved because P_1 was lost and P_2 learned from P_1's bad example, and so forth), which my explanation denies.

Indeed, it seems that God is acting as a deontologist, treating each person as an end in themselves rather than a mere means. God gives each person the good of his repletive presence, the faculty of libertarian free will, and his supreme respect for their choices. As J. P. Moreland points out, forcing people to go to heaven who do not want to experience the beatific

---

13. Manis, *Sinners*, 132.

The Relationship between Molinism and Eventual Universalism

vision is the course of action that would actually make God a consequentialist and that would constitute an immoral violation of their free choice:

> When you treat people as instrumentally valuable, or only as a means to an end, you're dehumanizing them, and that's wrong. . . . You only respect people when you treat them as having intrinsic value. . . . If you were to force people to do something against their free choice, you would be dehumanizing them. You would be saying that the good of what you want to do is more valuable than respecting their choices, and so you're treating people as a means to an end by requiring them to do something they don't want. That's what it would be like if God forced everyone to go to heaven. . . . The option of forcing everyone to go to heaven is immoral, because it's dehumanizing: it strips them of the dignity of making their own decision; it denies them their freedom of choice; and it treats them as a means to an end. . . . God respects human freedom. In fact, it would be unloving—a sort of divine rape—to force people to accept heaven and God if they didn't really want them. When God allows people to say "no" to him, he actually respects and dignifies them.[14]

At this point Manis could retort that my proposal, while logically possible, is highly improbable. I would respond that finite humans are in no epistemic position to assess the probability of such a proposal, making any probability estimate inscrutable. Hence there exist no grounds for judging my proposal highly improbable or even improbable at all. For these reasons, it seems that any objections Manis might levy against my model of NFUW *simpliciter* fail.

Manis now turns to the second version of NFUW, namely, NFUW with transworld damnation.[15] According to the theory of transworld damnation, the only people eternally damned in the actual world would be freely damned in every feasible world, and their existence (but not damnation) is required for anyone who would be saved to exist. Moreover, in

---

14. Moreland and Strobel, "Loving God," 182–83.

15. To be precise, Manis treats NFUW with transworld damnation and the additional claim "that there is no feasible world in all which all are saved and heaven is sufficiently populated" (*Sinners*, 133). Since I concur with Manis's intuition that it would be better for God to create a world in which all are saved and heaven is insufficiently populated than a world in which only some are saved and heaven is sufficiently populated (*Sinners*, 130–31), and since I deny that there is any feasible world in which all are saved and heaven is insufficiently populated, I need not append the additional claim to the model under discussion here.

Molinist Philosophical and Theological Ventures

God's providence, God ensures that any person in the actual world who is freely saved in any feasible world winds up being freely saved in the actual world. Manis admits that, on this version, God would not sacrifice anyone and that it is logically possible for this version to be true. However, he finds this version "simply incredible."[16] He insists that Molinists must believe this version not merely to be logically possible but also to be actual. For only if this version is actual does it succeed as a theodicy.[17] I do not grant this point, as it seems to me that a theodicy must only be logically possible and not highly improbable to succeed. But even if I granted this point, I fail to see why this version needs to be a theodicy rather than a defense, which indisputably requires at best the conjunction of logical possibility and the lack of high improbability. And the probability of this version, like that of NFUW *simpliciter*, is inscrutable, such that we have no reason to believe it is intrinsically improbable. As William Lane Craig writes,

> Since a world providentially ordered by God in the way I suggest would appear outwardly identical to a world in which one's birth is a matter of historical and geographical accident, it's hard to see how the hypothesis I've defended can be said to be improbable—apart from a demonstration that the existence of a God endowed with such knowledge [i.e., middle knowledge] is implausible. And I don't know of any such demonstration.[18]

Hence NFUW with transworld damnation survives Manis's critique.

We now turn to Reitan's claim that the doctrine of libertarian freedom essential to Molinism (which he calls radical libertarian freedom) guarantees the truth of eventual universalism. My best construction of his argument for this claim runs as follows.

1. Libertarian freedom contains a random element.
2. This random element does or does not extend to salvific choices.
3. If this random element does not cover salvific choices, then all persons will eventually be saved.
4. Mathematically, any random event with a nonzero probability will eventually happen given enough time.

---

16. Manis, *Sinners*, 133.
17. Manis, *Sinners*, 134.
18. Craig, *On Guard*, 282.

The Relationship between Molinism and Eventual Universalism

5. Given libertarian freedom, choosing to embrace God always has a nonzero probability.
6. If the random element in libertarian freedom covers salvific choices, then all persons will eventually be saved. (4, 5)
7. Therefore, eventual universalism is necessitated by libertarian freedom. (2, 3, 6)[19]

The controversial premises in this argument are (1) and (3). Notice here that (4) only applies to *random* events with nonzero probabilities; mathematically, a nonrandom event with a nonzero intrinsic probability may well fail to happen despite infinite time. For nonrandom events, the detachment rule for probabilities, which holds that a proposition *p* may be properly inferred from a high intrinsic probability for *p*, does not apply.[20] Neither does the agglomeration step apply to nonrandom events. The agglomeration step takes us from a high intrinsic probability of some event (e.g., that some person will eventually be saved) to a high intrinsic probability of the conjunction of all similar events (e.g., that all persons will eventually be saved). Even if we could infer that eventual salvation of a particular individual will nonrandomly obtain, we cannot validly conclude that the eventual salvation of every individual will nonrandomly obtain.[21] As Jonathan Kvanvig points out, even in random cases "it is rare for the probability of a conjunction to be as high for a conjunction as for the conjuncts."[22] It is especially rare in nonrandom cases.

Now consider (1). Libertarian freedom presupposes agent causation, a view dating back to Aristotle (384–322 BCE), Epicurus (341–270 BCE), and Carneades (214–129 BCE).[23] Agent causation holds, in Roderick Chisholm's words, that

> each of us, when we act, is a prime mover unmoved. In doing what we do, we cause certain events to happen, and nothing—or no one—causes us to cause those events to happen. If we are thus prime movers unmoved and if our actions, or those for which we are responsible, are not causally determined, then they are not

---

19. Reitan, "Guarantee of Universal Salvation," 419–24.
20. Kvanvig, *Destiny and Deliberation*, 23–24; Perszyk, "Open Theism," 171–72.
21. Kvanvig, *Destiny and Deliberation*, 24; Perszyk, "Open Theism," 172.
22. Kvanvig, *Destiny and Deliberation*, 24.
23. Doyle, "Agent-Causality."

causally determined by our *desires* . . . beliefs, and stimulus situation at any time.[24]

Aristotle, Epicurus, and Carneades contended that every event is brought about by one of three causes: necessity, chance (i.e., randomness), and agency. For them, agency constitutes a *tertium quid* that, by definition, is mutually exclusive with randomness. If human actions are brought about by either necessity or randomness, then humans are not responsible for their actions. However, humans possess "the autonomous ability to transcend necessity and chance . . . so that praise and blame are appropriate."[25] Eventual universalists like Thomas Talbott and Robin Parry argue that no one can make what Talbott first called a "fully informed decision" to reject God's saving grace.[26] It is important to observe that what eternalists would describe as a "fully informed decision" is quite different than what eventual universalists mean by this same term. Parry notes "that by 'fully informed' I do not simply mean that a person has had enough information communicated to them. I also mean that this information is *epistemically compelling* for them . . . the information is *imparted in a compelling way that elicits belief*."[27] Since the person lacks "the ability to refrain from exerting his power" to make such a decision,[28] Parry maintains that a fully informed decision is not a libertarian free decision.[29] Talbott concurs, explaining that the "compelling evidence" necessary for a fully informed decision "both justifies a belief and removes one's power on some occasion to reject the given belief."[30] Thus libertarian freedom, if true, rules out the possibility of God's fully informing someone in the sense meant by eventual universalists. I contend that being fully informed in this sense only occurs when one experiences the beatific vision, as experiencing the beatific vision seals a person in their pre-heavenly decision to choose God and thus removes their freedom to sin. In Reitan's words, I think that "experience of the beatific vision is *the only way* to wash away *all* ignorance, deception, and

---

24. Chisholm, "Human Freedom," 434–35.
25. Doyle, "Agent-Causality."
26. Talbott, *Inescapable Love*, 172–73; Parry, *Evangelical Universalist*, 28–29.
27. Parry, *Evangelical Universalist*, 29n45.
28. Moreland and Craig, *Philosophical Foundations*, 303, point out that this ability is a *sine qua non* for libertarian freedom.
29. Parry, *Evangelical Universalist*, 29–30.
30. Talbott, *Inescapable Love*, 202.

The Relationship between Molinism and Eventual Universalism

bondage to desire,"[31] since ignorance, deception, and/or bondage to desire can be chosen by a libertarian free agent.

But what if God fully informed, in the eternalist sense, each inhabitant of hell? On the eternalist sense, to be fully informed means to be aware of all the relevant evidence, to be able to judge it impartially, and to have "all salvation inhibitors ... removed *except those that cannot be removed short of experiencing the beatific vision.*"[32] Would being so informed and yet rejecting God show that, contra Aristotle, Epicurus, and Carneades, libertarian freedom contains a random element? Reitan answers "yes" to this question, while libertarians reply "no."[33] It seems that the varying answers point to different proposed relationships between freedom, reasons, and randomness. Reitan believes that any free decision not ultimately grounded on the basis of reasons, including beliefs, motives, feelings, and desires, is random:

> It takes freedom to involve an act of *choosing* among motives, and it is fair to ask why we would choose one motive rather than another. What motivates the choice of motives? Nothing? If so, then our choices turn out ... to be random. But if there is something that influences our choice of motives, what would that be? Some second-order motives, we might say.... Either our selection of it is random, or our selection of this motive is explained by the fact that we have *chosen* to have our choice of second-order motives be determined by an irrational third-order motive. But then this choice needs to be explained. The only escape from an infinite regress here is to posit a random element operating in human choice.[34]

To the contrary, the libertarian insists that, for a free decision not to be random, "the agent as a substance" simply needs to be "in control of his actions."[35] Agent causation guarantees that this condition is met for libertarian free agents. When a libertarian agent has a reason for acting, it is the agent *qua* first cause who chooses the reason, such that no infinite regress materializes. The agent is the ultimate ground of any reason for which the agent may act. And a libertarian agent may choose to act without any

---

31. Reitan, "Guarantee of Universal Salvation," 417.
32. Reitan, "Guarantee of Universal Salvation," 420.
33. Reitan, "Guarantee of Universal Salvation," 420; Craig, "Talbott's Universalism Once More," 501–2.
34. Reitan, "Guarantee of Universal Salvation," 418–19.
35. Moreland and Craig, *Philosophical Foundations*, 311.

reason. To misunderstand these facts, claims the libertarian, constitutes a failure to comprehend the notion of agent causation.

On the eternalist sense, then, a fully informed inhabitant of hell possessing libertarian freedom knows that God wills supreme happiness for the agent, which will only come upon experiencing the beatific vision. As Craig perceives, such a person, "out of a desire for self-autonomy," may "refus[e] even supreme happiness because its price—bowing the knee to God—is too high. Why could not someone's hatred of God be so implacable that he choose to reject God rather than be supremely happy?"[36] Such a person is "*self-deceived*," and it does not lie within God's omnipotence, "to destroy such self-deceptions without destroying such persons' freedom. For self-deception, being rooted in the free will of the creature, may be as impenetrable to God's grace as the free will itself. . . . God's removal of the deception in some persons could require abrogation of the freedom of the will itself, the freedom to deceive oneself."[37] Craig also insists, correctly in my judgment, that "perhaps no motivation is necessary for the decision to reject God."[38] A decision to "do wrong for its own sake and spurn God just to spurn Him" is not akin to a compulsion "like a drug addiction" or a random event like "a quantum leap" because "the decision arises from agent causation."[39] Any bondage experienced by someone making this kind of decision "is a self-bondage, rooted in their own will," and for such slavery they alone are morally liable.[40] Thus God cannot unbind them without removing their libertarian freedom to bind themselves and remain bound.

So is the libertarian correct that actions caused by an agent as a substance, even when not ultimately grounded on the basis of reasons, are not random? I believe an affirmative answer to this question can be demonstrated. Suppose *arguendo* that the eventual universalist is correct. If so, it is highly likely that there is more than one feasible world in which eventual universalism obtains; indeed, there is probably an infinite range of such worlds. Suppose all such worlds are equally good. Which one, if any, will God choose? I say "if any" because, even though it is better for any potential creature to be actualized than not, it is not better *per se* for an eventual universalist feasible world to be actualized than not. For, logically prior to

36. Craig, "Talbott's Universalism Once More," 501.
37. Craig, "Talbott's Universalism Once More," 501.
38. Craig, "Talbott's Universalism Once More," 501.
39. Craig, "Talbott's Universalism Once More," 502.
40. Craig, "Talbott's Universalism Once More," 502.

The Relationship between Molinism and Eventual Universalism

creation, God already existed in a perfect community of self-giving love among the three persons of the Trinity. Creating a world neither adds to nor subtracts from God's goodness, which is already maximal. Hence it seems that God's choice to create a feasible world where eventual universalism obtains is not ultimately grounded on the basis of reasons, including beliefs, motives, feelings, and desires. Rather, it is ultimately grounded in God, full stop. Would Manis therefore hold that God's choice to create an eventual universalist world is random? Surely not; such a conclusion would be absurd. Via *reductio*, then, it follows that actions caused by an agent as a substance, even when not ultimately grounded on the basis of reasons, are not random. Hence libertarian freedom does not include a random element, making (1) in Reitan's argument false.

What about (3), which states that if the random element in libertarian freedom does not cover salvific choices, then all persons will eventually be saved? Since there is no random element in libertarian freedom, no such element covers salvific choices. So is it true that a libertarian freedom sans randomness entails universal salvation? Mathematics is of no assistance in answering this question, since a nonrandom event with a nonzero intrinsic probability may indeed fail to happen given infinite time. I believe our question should be answered in the negative, in view of what Talbott dubs psychological impossibility. As two examples of psychological impossibility, Talbott offers "the loving mother who finds it utterly unthinkable ... to abandon her beloved baby" and "the honest banker who" refuses "to accept a bribe."[41] Recall that the intrinsic probability of each of these events is its "prior probability arising from its content alone and independent of all evidence."[42] Such evidence includes the facts of human psychology. Accordingly, the libertarian freedom enjoyed by the mother and the banker render the respective intrinsic probabilities of choosing to stop being loving and abandon the baby or choosing to stop being honest and accept the bribe as nonzero. Suppose Talbott accepted libertarian freedom (which he does not).[43] Then it seems Talbott would have to conclude, consistent with his argument, that the mother would never choose to stop being loving and abandon the baby and the baker would never choose to stop being honest

---

41. Talbott, *Inescapable Love*, 198.

42. Swinburne, *Epistemic Justification*, 138n12.

43. Talbott, *Inescapable Love*, 198 writes: "But the concept of *libertarian freedom*, insofar as it requires the power of contrary choice, nonetheless seems to me an artificial philosophical construction, one that in some contexts at least seems inconsistent with our ordinary paradigms of free action."

and accept the bribe even given infinite opportunities to do so and even though they could (i.e., it is logically possible for them to) do so. Notice, given libertarian freedom, that psychological impossibility is self-imposed (imposed by free choice) and not logically imposed. Likewise, there may be some hateful persons who could freely, but would never, choose to stop hating God and repent of their sins. As I have already suggested, there may be some autonomous persons who could freely, but would never, choose theonomy rather than autonomy and some evil persons who could freely, but would never, abandon doing evil for evil's sake. Consequently, it is a self-imposed psychological impossibility for such persons to embrace God. God cannot remove this psychological impossibility, which is freely chosen, without taking away their libertarian freedom. Hence a libertarian freedom sans randomness does not entail universal salvation, making (3) false as well.

Given the failure of Manis's argument that eternalism is improbable and of Reitan's argument that libertarian freedom renders eventual universalism necessary, we may conclude that Molinism shows eternalism to be logically possible and not necessarily improbable.

Molinism and Eventual Universalism

It is rather straightforward to establish that Molinism shows eventual universalism to be logically possible. Suppose God knows in his middle knowledge that there are feasible worlds where all eventually embrace God, either on earth or in hell. If there are such worlds, an all-loving God would, in my judgment, create one if he decides to create a world at all. This observation establishes eventual universalism's logical possibility. On Molinism, moreover, the probability that there exists a feasible world where all eventually embrace God is inscrutable and therefore not necessarily improbable. Accordingly, Ken Perszyk claims that "Molinism is well suited for universalism,"[44] which concurs with Parry's judgment that Molinism "fit[s] very well with universalism."[45] Indeed, Manis notes that "Molinism and universalism would seem to be a match made in heaven."[46] However, I wish to go further. I shall now argue that, given libertarian freedom, Molinism furnishes the only way God could guarantee universal salvation. To make

44. Perszyk, "Open Theism," 169.
45. Parry, *Evangelical Universalist*, 28.
46. Manis, *Sinners*, 123.

The Relationship between Molinism and Eventual Universalism

this case, I need to show that God could not guarantee universal salvation on the other two views subscribing to libertarian freedom, namely, simple foreknowledge and open theism.

Simple foreknowledge could be paired with either an A-Theory or B-Theory of time. On the A-Theory, God possesses only natural knowledge logically prior to his creative decision. As I argued in chapter 5, would-probably counterfactuals comprise part of this knowledge. For God naturally knows the intrinsic probability of each counterfactual of creaturely freedom (CCF). But because the CCFs are non-random, God cannot detach, or infer, any CCF from its high intrinsic probability. Lacking middle knowledge, God cannot choose any feasible world he wants. Recalling my conception of "possible galaxy" from chapter 6, God can only choose the possible galaxy, or trunk of the tree, that will eventuate in the actual world upon God's creative decision. The various branches include the various ways God could freely act in the world. Hence when selecting a possible galaxy, God can at best pick some candidate with the highest intrinsic probability of resulting in a world featuring eventual universalism. However, this intrinsic probability, a conjunction including many non-random events (i.e., CCFs), is also non-random, furnishing God with no evidence that eventual universalism will obtain. Upon God's choice, God learns the thin red line of the galaxy, discovering what creatures will exist and how both they and he will act in the world. As indicated by the various scriptural texts depicting divine confrontation of the unexpected, God finds himself on simple foreknowledge extremely surprised as to what he foreknows. Indeed, God was shocked that the antediluvian world degenerated into utter violence and depravity and wished that he had never chosen to create a world at all (Gen 6:5–6)! Consequently, we can repose no confidence that the actual world will achieve eventual universalism on simple foreknowledge conjoined with the A-Theory. If the world indeed achieves eventual universalism, it would simply be a matter of dumb luck.

The situation gets even worse on the B-Theory. For the actual world, eternally existing as a four-dimensional spacetime block, is plausibly not even chosen by God. It is hard to see how the world could have been created by God *ex nihilo*. It rather seems that any doctrine of creation is reduced to *creatio continuans*, whereby the world is ontologically dependent on God in the same way as are laws of logic, numbers, and objective moral values—none of which God wills to exist—and is sustained by God in being.[47] In

---

47. Moreland and Craig, *Philosophical Foundations*, 557–59; Craig, *Time and Eternity*, 212–13.

the words of prominent B-Theorist Brian Leftow, "So if God is timeless and a world or time exists, there is no phase of His life during which He is without a world or time or has not yet decided to create them ... the universe is in eternity just the timeless obtaining of a causal dependence or sustaining relation between God and a world whose time has a first moment."[48] The B-Theory entails that God possesses natural knowledge logically simultaneous with his foreknowledge, as the two species of knowledge are derived in radically different ways. God's natural knowledge is conceptualist, while his foreknowledge is perceptualist. In other words, God's natural knowledge is innate and contained within his own mind, while God's foreknowledge is a matter of his looking out, so to speak, at the block universe to see what happens at every point on the timeline.[49] It is like someone sitting on a mountaintop and observing at once everything that happens from horizon to horizon.[50] Since God has no control over what his foreknowledge would include, he has no control over what kind of world he has to work with. Assuming that his foreknowledge includes knowledge of his own actions, sans any creative decision God does not seem to choose how he will act toward humanity, such that God's libertarian freedom toward humans is sacrificed on the altar of human libertarian freedom. Thus God has no guarantee or even reasonable prospect that any of his ventures, given human libertarian freedom, to achieve eventual universalism will succeed.

Recognizing the problems posed by the B-Theory, open theists are firmly committed to an A-Theory of time. Open theism acknowledges God's prevolitional knowledge of the intrinsic probability of each CCF but denies God's middle knowledge of CCFs themselves. Some open theists, most notably Gregory Boyd and Elijah Hess, redefine God's middle knowledge so as to comprise these intrinsic probabilities, such that God has middle knowledge of might, but not would, counterfactuals.[51] Like A-Theorist simple foreknowledge, open theism maintains that God chooses not a feasible world but a possible galaxy. However, unlike A-Theorist simple foreknowledge, God does not decide in his creative decision the various ways he will act in the future, but he does decide how he would act

---

48. Leftow, *Time and Eternity*, 290–91, as quoted in Craig, *Time and Eternity*, 213.

49. Craig explains the difference between conceptualist and perceptualist notions of divine knowledge in "Middle-Knowledge View," 133.

50. Boethius, *Consolation of Philosophy* 5.6.15–43; see also Craig, *Time and Eternity*, 111–12.

51. Boyd, "Neo-Molinism," 192–94; Hess, "Arguing," 335–36, 351.

The Relationship between Molinism and Eventual Universalism

in any conceivable circumstances.[52] This is because God's creative decision does not afford God knowledge of the galaxy's thin red line. Indeed the galaxy does not yet have a thin red line, for the galaxy is open to all possible branches that might emanate from its trunk. Hence God does not know future contingents regarding human freedom, but he is prepared to react to anything humans might do. God and humans dynamically interact within the world, in which God, infinitely superior to a chess grandmaster, takes the calculated risks he has already decided upon to achieve his aims. Due to God's infinite resourcefulness, open theists hold that God will eventually accomplish all his goals.

But can the combination of calculated risk-taking and infinite resourcefulness guarantee eventual universalism? Based on the fact that probability rules needed for this guarantee fail to apply to non-random events like CCFs, the answer seems to be no. On a noncompulsory, *prima facie* account of a fully informed free decision, open theism does not, contra Talbott, render, in Perszyk's words, "incoherent... the idea of a person making a fully informed free decision against God."[53] Perszyk goes on to point out that open theists hold to a libertarianism which "seems to recognize that even when there is no good reason or motivation to refrain from doing something, and every reason or motivation to do it, we could (must) still be able to do otherwise."[54] Notice that, due to agent causation, such a libertarianism would not contain a random element. Hence perfect knowledge of intrinsic probabilities and infinite resourcefulness are insufficient on open theism to secure eventual universalism. Since open theism precludes the idea of God's knowing that eventual universalism will obtain, it also, interestingly, precludes God, owing to his veracity, from revealing in Scripture that all will be saved. So if open theism is true, then the interpretation of the scriptural texts marshaled by eventual universalists cannot be correct. For this reason alone, I think, no eventual universalist should be an open theist.

Since neither simple foreknowledge nor open theism furnishes any guarantee that all actual libertarian persons will eventually be saved, the only model that could afford such a guarantee is Molinism. For suppose God middle-knows that there are some feasible worlds where all are eventually freely saved, one of which God in his omnibenevolence would choose

---

52. Hess, "Arguing," 336.
53. Perszyk, "Open Theism," 170.
54. Perszyk, "Open Theism," 170.

to create. If and only if this is true, God could scripturally reveal that all are eventually freely saved. This is precisely what eventual universalists insist. In my judgment, then, the only hope for eventual universalism is Molinism.

Conclusion

On a Molinist account, eternalism and eventual universalism are each logically possible and not necessarily improbable. Either option could be true, yet neither option is necessarily true. Thus I agree with the sentiment of Perszyk:

> Molinism does not by itself entail that some persons will freely reject God and be lost, nor does it entail that all will freely accept and be saved.... But given its commitment to libertarianism, it seems that Molinists cannot deliver necessary universalism—the thesis that it is logically necessary that all will (eventually) be saved—but only contingent universalism (i.e., as a matter of fact all will be saved). This also assumes that freely accepting God is required for salvation. However, even if contingent universalism were the best that God can do under Molinism, he would know prior to creation that all persons would (will) be saved. It would thus be something he could reveal in Scripture, which defenders of universalism presumably believe has been done.[55]

Given Molinism, then, the matter of whether eternalism or eventual universalism is true can only be decided on scriptural grounds; philosophical considerations do not apply.[56] To be clear, I am an eternalist myself. But I would encourage readers to consult the works in the following footnote and make up their own minds on this issue based on their assessment of the biblical evidence.[57] The jointly necessary and sufficient pillars of Molinism are middle knowledge and libertarian freedom.[58] Only if either pillar were false, rendering Molinism false, would philosophical arguments for eternalism or eventual universalism enter the argumentative fray.

---

55. Perszyk, "Open Theism," 169.

56. Of course, Molinism could be challenged on either biblical or philosophical grounds; if such challenges were successful, then philosophical considerations would apply to the debate between eternalism and eventual universalism.

57. For the biblical case for eternalism, see Shedd, *Endless Punishment*; Peterson, *Hell on Trial*; for the biblical case for eventual universalism, see Parry, *Evangelical Universalist*; Talbott, *Inescapable Love*.

58. Stratton and Erasmus, "Mere Molinism," 18.

Conclusion

THIS BOOK HAS ATTEMPTED to defend Molinism from both perennial and new challenges and to reveal the power of Molinism to shed light on divine intuition, biblical passages portraying divine relational changeability, branching time models, the relationship between music and apologetics, and the prospect of eventual universalism. The opening two chapters argue that Molinism is not imposed on the Bible but is rather derived from the Bible and provides the best explanation of various categories of scriptural texts that have historically been regarded as in tension with one another.[1] The explanation Molinism furnishes is clear and convincing, not subordinating any doctrinal locus to another but allowing each to be maintained at face value. Such loci include divine sovereignty, human freedom, predestination, grace, and God's universal salvific will. After surveying the proffered responses to the grounding objection, the third chapter contends, in interdisciplinary fashion, that intuition is best understood as a cognitive faculty that affords judgment in eventually underdeterminative cases. From the observation that human intuition, as part of the *imago Dei*, is generally reliable, we may reason by analogy that the divine intuition is completely reliable. God's intuited beliefs about counterfactuals of creaturely freedom (CCFs) constitute their truthmakers, thus yielding a novel answer to the

---

1. Indeed, Molina constructed his model by starting from the text of Scripture and systematizing its doctrines of grace, foreknowledge, providence, predestination, reprobation, and human freedom in book one of the *Concordia*, and only then proceeding philosophically in books two through seven.

grounding objection. The fourth chapter contests the recent explanatory priority arguments against Molinism offered by Philip Swenson, Nevin Climenhaga, and Daniel Rubio. Contra Swenson, Molinism is shown not to exhibit a vicious circularity. Contra Swenson, Climenhaga, and Rubio, Molinism is shown not to unwittingly destroy libertarian human freedom. Indeed there is no explanatory relation between CCFs and free creaturely actions, but rather there exists an acausal, i.e., noninfluential, symmetry between them.

The fifth and sixth chapters hold significant implications for appraising the Stalnaker-Lewis semantics for counterfactuals exploited by open theists. Contrary to the semantics, might-counterfactuals are seen not to be the contradictories of would-counterfactuals (which I regard as the only type of counterfactuals, properly speaking) but rather as statements of intrinsic probability, namely, that the intrinsic probability of an event's actual occurrence under the relevant circumstances is greater than some very low probability (e.g., .1). For well-formed counterfactuals, the law of conditional excluded middle (CEM) holds, such that the contradictory of $x \;\Box\!\!\rightarrow y$ is $x \;\Box\!\!\rightarrow \sim y$, not $x \;\Diamond\!\!\rightarrow \sim y$.[2] These findings substantiate Marcus Arvan's recent refutation of the Stalnaker-Lewis semantics in general.[3] The fifth chapter applies Molinism to exegete divine relational changeability texts as either metaphors for timeless relations of logical order or literal depictions of divine emotions which were counterbalanced by other divine emotions. The sixth chapter shows how Molinism affords an illuminating account of branching time models, understood non-literally as heuristic devices, as illustrating the relationship between possible galaxies, possible futures, feasible futures, and feasible worlds. Here I should point out that branching time models give the lie to the open theist allegation that there is a logical distinction between the locutions "x will not" and not [x will]," such that the latter means "x might" rather than "x will not." According to open theists, then, the contradictory of "x will" is "x might not" and the contradictory of "x will not" is "x might."[4] This only follows if one presupposes the tenets of the Stalnaker-Lewis semantics already shown to be

2. The $\Box\!\!\rightarrow$ operator stands for "if the antecedent were the case, then the consequent would be the case," and the $\Diamond\!\!\rightarrow$ operator stands for "if the antecedent were the case, then the consequent might be the case." See Williams, "Defending," for what I consider an outstanding defense of conditional excluded middle.

3. Arvan, "Refutation," 109–29.

4. Boyd, "Motivations," 46–47; Hess, "Arguing," 332; Hess, "Has Molina Collapsed," 392–96.

Conclusion

false.⁵ But in branching time models, there simply are no "might" branches on the trees. They picture the reality, identified by Carneades, that "not [x will]" is logically equivalent to "x will not."⁶

The seventh chapter furnishes a Molinist account of holy music, according to which God suffuses music with his presence upon his middle knowledge that, were God to do so, the *sensus divinitatis* of at least one performer or hearer would function properly and at least one of these same performers of hearers would freely respond to the output of the *sensus divinitatis* and enter into relationship with God. In this case, music plays a powerful apologetic role. Indeed the expansion of Molinism into the realm of aesthetics represents a significant advance. The eighth chapter reveals that Molinism is consistent with the eternalist view of hell and with eventual universalism, rendering both possible and neither improbable. Moreover, assuming the truth of libertarian freedom, Molinism offers the sole model on which eventual universalism is possible.

This book, in sum, represents an array of the ways Molinism can be defended and expanded into further areas of philosophy and theology. In view of the biblical foundations and conceptual power of Molinism, it is my hope and endeavor that such philosophical and theological ventures will continue to attract scholarly attention.

---

5. Hess, "Arguing," 341; Hess, "Has Molina Collapsed," 392. As William Lane Craig rightly observes regarding the aforementioned open theist allegation, "the problem with this is that it mixes modal locutions ('might' statements) with nonmodal locutions ('will' statements). In normal English, the statement that something will occur, but might not occur, is perfectly coherent. That is just to affirm that it will happen contingently" ("Response to Boyd," 229).

6. That Carneades made this identification is pointed out by Boyd ("Motivations," 43), who rejects Carneades' view in favor of Aristotle's view depicted in his Square of Opposition ("Motivations," 46–47). However, as Lorenz Demey rightly warns, "In the theoretical investigation of Aristotelian diagrams, it is well-known that these diagrams are highly 'sensitive' to the underlying logical system, i.e., to one's logical assumptions. . . . The analysis in this paper shows that the same also holds for one's philosophical assumptions (in particular, regarding the question whether or not 'might and might not' constitutes a genuine ontological possibility). It would be naïve to presume that Aristotelian diagrams can, by themselves, lead to a definitive solution of this philosophical debate" ("Aristotelian Diagrams," 328).

Bibliography

Abasciano, Brian J. "Corporate Election in Romans 9: A Reply to Thomas Schreiner." *Journal of the Evangelical Theological Society* 49 (2006) 351–71.
———. *Paul's Use of the Old Testament in Romans 9.1–9: An Intertextual and Theological Exegesis*. London: T. & T. Clark, 2006.
———. *Paul's Use of the Old Testament in Romans 9.10–18: An Intertextual and Theological Exegesis*. London: T. & T. Clark, 2013.
Adams, Robert Merrihew. "An Anti-Molinist Argument." *Philosophical Perspectives* 5 (1991) 343–53.
———. "Middle Knowledge and the Problem of Evil." *American Philosophical Quarterly* 14 (1977) 109–17.
Alston, William P. "Does God Have Beliefs?" *Religious Studies* 22 (1986) 287–306.
Aquinas, Thomas. *Summa Theologiae*. Translated by the Fathers of the English Dominican Province. New York: Benzinger Brothers, 1947–48.
Armstrong, D. M. *Truth and Truthmakers*. Cambridge: Cambridge University Press, 2004.
Arvan, Marcus. "A Refutation of the Lewis-Stalnaker Account of Counterfactuals." *Metaphysica* 17 (2016) 109–29.
Augustine. *Against Julian*. Translated by Matthew A. Schuhmacher. The Fathers of the Church 35. Washington, DC: Catholic University of America Press, 1957.
———. *Against Two Letters of the Pelagians*. In *Nicene and Post-Nicene Fathers, First Series*, edited by Philip Schaff, translated by Peter Holmes and Robert Ernest Wallis, revised by Benjamin B. Warfield, 5:373–434. Reprint, Peabody, MA: Hendrickson, 1994.
———. *Enchiridion*. In *Nicene and Post-Nicene Fathers, First Series*, edited by Philip Schaff, translated by J. F. Shaw, 3:229–76. Reprint, Peabody, MA: Hendrickson, 1994.
———. *Letters of St. Augustin*. In *Nicene and Post-Nicene Fathers, First Series*, edited by Philip Schaff, translated by J. G. Cunningham, 1:209–593. Reprint, Peabody, MA: Hendrickson, 1994.

Bibliography

———. *On Man's Perfection in Righteousness*. In *Nicene and Post-Nicene Fathers, First Series*, edited by Philip Schaff, translated by Peter Holmes and Robert Ernest Wallis, revised by Benjamin B. Warfield, 5:153–76. Reprint, Peabody, MA: Hendrickson, 1994.

Barth, Karl. *Church Dogmatics*. Edited by G. W. Bromiley and Thomas F. Torrance. Translated by G. T. Thomson and Harold Knight. 4 vols. Edinburgh: T. & T. Clark, 1956–75.

Basil of Caesarea. "Homily on the First Psalm." In *Source Readings in Music History from Classical Antiquity through the Romantic Era*, edited by Oliver Strunk, 64–66. New York: Norton, 1950.

Basinger, David. "Practical Implications." In *The Openness of God: A Biblical Challenge to the Traditional Understanding of God*, by Clark Pinnock et al., 155–76. Downers Grove, IL: InterVarsity, 1994.

Bates, Matthew W. *Salvation by Allegiance Alone: Rethinking Faith, Works, and the Gospel of Jesus the King*. Grand Rapids: Baker Academic, 2017.

Bauer, Walter, et al. *A Greek-English Lexicon of the New Testament and Other Early Christian Literature*. 2nd ed. Chicago: University of Chicago Press, 1979.

Begbie, Jeremy S. "Faithful Feelings: Music and Emotion in Worship." In *Resonant Witness: Conversations between Music and Theology*, edited by Jeremy S. Begbie and Steven R. Guthrie, 323–54. Grand Rapids: Eerdmans, 2011.

Belnap, Nuel. "An Indeterminist View of the Parameters of Truth." In *Philosophie der Zeit: Neue Analytische Ansätze*, edited by Thomas Müller, 87–113. Frankfurt am Main: Klostermann, 2007.

Bengson, John. "Experimental Attacks on Intuitions and Answers." *Philosophy and Phenomenological Research* 86 (2013) 495–532.

———. "The Intellectual Given." *Mind* 124 (2015) 707–60.

Bigelow, John. *The Reality of Numbers: A Physicalist's Philosophy of Mathematics*. Oxford: Clarendon, 1988.

Boersma, Hans. *Five Things Theologians Wish Biblical Scholars Knew*. Downers Grove, IL: IVP Academic, 2021.

Boethius. *The Consolation of Philosophy*. Translated by Victor Watts. Rev. ed. New York: Penguin, 1999.

Booth, Anthony Robert, and Daniel P. Rowbottom, eds. *Intuitions*. Oxford: Oxford University Press, 2014.

Boyd, Gregory A. "Christian Love and Academic Dialogue: A Reply to Bruce Ware." *Journal of the Evangelical Theological Society* 45 (2002) 233–43.

———. "Neo-Molinism and the Infinite Intelligence of God." *Philosophia Christi* 5 (2003) 188–204.

———. "An Open-Theism Response [to the Middle-Knowledge View]." In *Divine Foreknowledge: Four Views*, edited by James K. Beilby and Paul R. Eddy, 144–48. Downers Grove, IL: InterVarsity, 2001.

———. "The Open-Theism View." In *Divine Foreknowledge: Four Views*, edited by James K. Beilby and Paul R. Eddy, 13–47. Downers Grove, IL: InterVarsity, 2001.

———. "Two Ancient (and Modern) Motivations for Ascribing Exhaustively Definite Foreknowledge to God: A Historic Overview and Critical Assessment." *Religious Studies* 46 (2010) 41–59.

Braüner, Torben, et al. "Determinism and the Origins of Temporal Logic." In *Advances in Temporal Logic*, edited by Howard Barringer et al., 185–206. Cham: Springer, 2000.

Bibliography

Brown, Francis, et al. *The Brown-Driver-Briggs Hebrew and English Lexicon*. Boston: Houghton and Mifflin, 1906.

Bultmann, Rudolf. *Jesus Christ and Mythology*. New York: Scribner, 1958.

Calvin, John. *Institutes of the Christian Religion*. Edited by John T. McNeill. Translated by Ford Lewis Battles. 2 vols. Philadelphia: Westminster, 1960.

———. *Preface to the Genevan Psalter*. In *Les Pseaumes mis en rime francoise par Clément Marot et Théodore de Béze. Mis en musique a quatre parties par Claude Goudimel. Par les héritiers de Francois Jacqui*, edited by Pierre Pidoux, translated by Charles Garside Jr., 1–4. Lausanne: La Société des Concerts de la Cathédrale de Lausanne, 1975.

Clement of Alexandria. *Pædagogus*. In *Ante-Nicene Fathers*, edited by Alexander Roberts and James Donaldson, translated by A. Cleveland Coxe, 2:207–96. Reprint, Peabody, MA: Hendrickson, 1994.

———. *Protrepticus*. In *Ante-Nicene Fathers*, edited by Alexander Roberts and James Donaldson, translated by A. Cleveland Coxe, 2:171–206. Reprint, Peabody, MA: Hendrickson, 1994.

Climenhaga, Nevin, and Daniel Rubio. "Molinism: Explaining Our Freedom Away." *Mind* 131 (2022) 459–85.

Chisholm, Roderick M. "Human Freedom and the Self." In *Philosophy: The Quest for Truth*, edited by Louis J. Pojman and Lewis Vaughn, 429–37. 9th ed. Oxford: Oxford University Press, 2014.

Collins, John J. *A Short Introduction to the Hebrew Bible*. Minneapolis: Fortress, 2007.

Craig, William Lane. *Divine Foreknowledge and Human Freedom: The Coherence of Theism: Omniscience*. Brill's Studies in Intellectual History 19. Leiden: Brill, 1991.

———. *Hard Questions, Real Answers*. Wheaton, IL: Crossway, 2003.

———. "Middle Knowledge, Truth-Makers, and the 'Grounding Objection.'" *Faith and Philosophy* 18 (2001) 337–52.

———. "A Middle-Knowledge Response [to the Open-Theism View]." In *Divine Foreknowledge: Four Views*, edited by James K. Beilby and Paul R. Eddy, 55–60. Downers Grove, IL: InterVarsity, 2001.

———. "The Middle-Knowledge View." In *Divine Foreknowledge: Four Views*, edited by James K. Beilby and Paul R. Eddy, 119–43. Downers Grove, IL: InterVarsity, 2001.

———. "'No Other Name': A Middle Knowledge Perspective on the Exclusivity of Salvation through Christ." *Faith and Philosophy* 6 (1989) 172–88.

———. *On Guard: Defending Your Faith with Reason and Precision*. Colorado Springs, CO: Cook, 2010.

———. "On Hasker's Defense of Anti-Molinism." *Faith and Philosophy* 15 (1998) 236–40.

———. *The Only Wise God: The Compatibility of Divine Foreknowledge and Human Freedom*. Grand Rapids: Baker, 1987.

———. *The Problem of Divine Foreknowledge and Future Contingents from Aristotle to Suarez*. Brill's Studies in Intellectual History 7. Leiden: Brill, 1988.

———. "Response to Gregory A. Boyd." In *Four Views on Divine Providence*, edited by Dennis W. Jowers, 224–30. Grand Rapids: Zondervan, 2011.

———. "Robert Adams's New Anti-Molinist Argument." *Philosophy and Phenomenological Research* 54 (1994) 857–61.

———. "Talbott's Universalism Once More." *Religious Studies* 29 (1993) 497–518.

———. *Time and Eternity: Exploring God's Relationship to Time*. Wheaton, IL: Crossway, 2001.

Bibliography

———. "Time and the Kalam Cosmological Argument." *Reasonable Faith*, May 6, 2012. https://www.reasonablefaith.org/writings/question-answer/time-and-the-kalam-cosmological-argument.

Cross, Charles B. "Conditional Excluded Middle." *Erkenntnis* 70 (2009) 173–88.

Demey, Lorenz. "Aristotelian Diagrams in the Debate on Future Contingents: A Methodological Reflection on Hess's Open Future Square of Opposition." *Sophia* 58 (2019) 321–29.

Dickinson, Travis M. "God Knows: Acquaintance and the Nature of Divine Knowledge." *Religious Studies* 55 (2019) 1–16.

Dörfler, Viktor, and Fran Ackermann. "Understanding Intuition: The Case for Two Forms of Intuition." *Management Science* 43 (2012) 545–64.

Doyle, Bob. "Agent-Causality." *The Information Philosopher*. https://www.informationphilosopher.com/freedom/agent-causality.html.

Durnbaugh, Donald F. *Fruit of the Vine: A History of the Brethren, 1708–1995*. Elgin, IL: Brethren, 1997.

Edgar, William. "Music." In *New Dictionary of Christian Apologetics*, edited by W. C. Campbell-Jack et al., 460–63. Downers Grove, IL: IVP Academic, 2006.

Egler, Miguel. "Testing for the Phenomenal: Intuition, Metacognition, and Philosophical Methodology." *Mind & Language* 35 (2020) 48–66.

Epstein, Richard L., with Michael Rooney. *Critical Thinking*. 4th ed. Sorocco, NM: Advanced Reasoning Forum, 2013.

Erickson, Millard J. *What Does God Know and When Does He Know It? The Current Controversy over Divine Foreknowledge*. Grand Rapids: Zondervan, 2006.

Flint, Thomas P. *Divine Providence: The Molinist Account*. Cornell Studies in the Philosophy of Religion. Ithaca, NY: Cornell University Press, 1998.

———. "A New Anti-Anti-Molinist Argument." *Religious Studies* 35 (1999) 299–305.

Flint, Thomas P., and Alfred J. Freddoso. "Maximal Power." In *The Existence and Nature of God*, edited by Alfred J. Freddoso, 81–114. Notre Dame: University of Notre Dame Press, 1983.

Gaskin, Richard. "Conditionals of Freedom and Middle Knowledge." *Philosophical Quarterly* 43 (1993) 412–30.

Grudem, Wayne. *Systematic Theology: An Introduction to Biblical Doctrine*. Grand Rapids: Zondervan, 1994.

Harrison, Everett F. "Romans." In *The Expositor's Bible Commentary*, edited by Frank E. Gæbelein, 10:1–171. Grand Rapids: Zondervan, 1976.

Hasker, William. "Anti-Molinism Is Undefeated!" *Faith and Philosophy* 17 (2000) 126–31.

———. "Explanatory Priority: Transitive and Unequivocal, a Reply to William Craig." *Philosophy and Phenomenological Research* 57 (1997) 389–93.

———. *God, Time, and Knowledge*. Cornell Studies in the Philosophy of Religion. Ithaca, NY: Cornell University Press, 1989.

———. "A New Anti-Molinist Argument." *Religious Studies* 35 (1999) 291–97.

Hays, Richard B. *The Conversion of the Imagination*. Grand Rapids: Eerdmans, 2005.

Hess, Elijah. "Arguing from Molinism to Neo-Molinism." *Philosophia Christi* 17 (2015) 331–51.

———. "Has Molina Collapsed the Neo-Molinist Square? A Rejoinder to Kirk MacGregor." *Philosophia Christi* 21 (2019) 391–406.

Bibliography

Johnson, Michael, and Jennifer Nado. "Moderate Intuitionism: A Metasemantic Account." In *Intuitions*, edited by Anthony Robert Booth and Darrell P. Rowbottom, 68–90. Oxford: Oxford University Press, 2014.

Kahneman, Daniel. *Thinking, Fast and Slow*. New York: Farrar, Straus, and Giroux, 2011.

Koksvik, Ole. "Intuition." PhD diss., Australian National University, 2011.

Kowalski, Dean A. "On Behalf of a Suarezian Middle Knowledge." *Philosophia Christi* 5 (2003) 219–28.

Kristjánsson, Kristján. *Aristotle, Emotions, and Education*. New York: Routledge, 2016.

Kvanvig, Jonathan L. *Destiny and Deliberation: Essays in Philosophical Theology*. Oxford: Oxford University Press, 2011.

———. *The Possibility of an All-Knowing God*. New York: Palgrave Macmillan, 1986.

Laing, John D. *Middle Knowledge: Human Freedom in Divine Sovereignty*. Grand Rapids: Kregel, 2018.

———. "Molinism and Supercomprehension: Grounding Counterfactual Truth." PhD diss., Southern Baptist Theological Seminary, 2000.

Law, Andrew. "From the Fixity of the Past to the Fixity of the Independent." *Philosophical Studies* 178 (2021) 1301–14.

Leftow, Brian. *Time and Eternity*. Cornell Studies in the Philosophy of Religion. Ithaca, NY: Cornell University Press, 1991.

Lewis, David. *Counterfactuals*. Library of Philosophy and Logic. Oxford: Blackwell, 1973.

Lewis, Gordon. "Impassibility of God." In *Evangelical Dictionary of Theology*, edited by Walter A. Elwell, 598–99. 2nd ed. Grand Rapids: Baker, 2001.

Louw, Johannes P., and Eugene A. Nida. *Greek-English Lexicon of the New Testament Based on Semantic Domains*. 2 vols. 2nd ed. New York: United Bible Societies, 1989.

Lowe, E. J. "What Is the Source of Our Knowledge of Modal Truths?" *Mind* 121 (2012) 919–50.

Luther, Martin. *The Bondage of the Will*. In *Martin Luther: Selections from His Writings*, edited by John Dillenberger, translated by J. I. Packer and A. R. Johnston, 166–203. New York: Anchor, 1962.

———. *The Freedom of a Christian*. In *Martin Luther: Selections from His Writings*, edited by John Dillenberger, translated by W. A. Lambert, revised by Harold J. Grimm, 42–85. New York: Anchor, 1962.

MacGregor, Kirk R. "Aquinas, Christology, and Art." *Bridges* 14 (2007) 233–50.

———. "The Existence and Irrelevance of Gratuitous Evil." *Philosophia Christi* 14 (2012) 165–80.

———. *A Historical and Theological Investigation of John's Gospel*. Cham: Palgrave Macmillan, 2020.

———. *Luis de Molina: The Life and Theology of the Founder of Middle Knowledge*. Grand Rapids: Zondervan, 2015.

———. *A Molinist-Anabaptist Systematic Theology*. Lanham, MD: University Press of America, 2007.

Mack, Alexander. *The Complete Writings of Alexander Mack*. Edited by William R. Eberly. Winona Lake, IN: BMH, 1991.

Malpass, Alex. "The Grounding Objection to Molinism—Dr. Kirk MacGregor & Dr. Alex Malpass." *YouTube*, December 16, 2019. https://www.youtube.com/watch?v=lwItJEK7nLs.

Malpass, Alex, and Jacek Wawer. "A Future for the Thin Red Line." *Synthese* 188 (2012) 117–42.

Bibliography

Manis, R. Zachary. *Sinners in the Presence of a Loving God: An Essay on the Problem of Hell*. Oxford: Oxford University Press, 2019.

Matava, R. J. *Divine Causality and Human Free Choice: Domingo Báñez, Physical Premotion, and the Controversy de Auxiliis Revisisted*. Brill's Studies in Intellectual History 252. Leiden: Brill, 2016.

McClymond, Michael, and Paul Copan. "How Univeralism, 'the Opiate of the Theologians,' Went Mainstream." *Christianity Today*, March 11, 2019. https://www.christianitytoday.com/ct/2019/march-web-only/michael-mcclymond-devils-redemption-universalism.html.

McKim, Vaughn R., and Charles C. Davis. "Temporal Modalities and the Future." *Notre Dame Journal of Formal Logic* 17 (1976) 233–38.

Milne, Peter. "Not Every Truth Has a Truthmaker." *Analysis* 65 (2005) 221–24.

Molina, Luis de. *Liberi Arbitrii cum Gratiae Donis, Divina Praescientia, Providentia, Praedestinatione et Reprobatione Concordia*. Edited by Johannes Rabeneck. Madrid: Soc. Edit. "Sapientia," 1953.

———. *On Divine Foreknowledge: Part IV of the Concordia*. Translated by Alfred J. Freddoso. Ithaca, NY: Cornell University Press, 1988.

Moreland, J. P. *The Soul: How We Know It's Real and Why It Matters*. Chicago: Moody, 2014.

Moreland, J. P., and Lee Strobel. "Objection #6: A Loving God Would Never Torture People in Hell." In *The Case for Faith: A Journalist Investigates the Toughest Objections to Christianity*, by Lee Strobel, 169–94. Grand Rapids: Zondervan, 2000.

Moreland, J. P., and William Lane Craig. *Philosophical Foundations for a Christian Worldview*. 2nd ed. Downers Grove, IL: IVP Academic, 2017.

Nagel, Jennifer. "Intuitions and Experiments: A Defense of the Case Method in Epistemology." *Philosophy and Phenomenological Research* 85 (2012) 495–527.

Øhrstrøm, Peter. "What William of Ockham and Luis de Molina Would Have Said to Nuel Belnap: A Discussion of Some Arguments against 'The Thin Red Line.'" In *Nuel Belnap on Indeterminism and Free Action*, edited by Thomas Müller, 175–90. Cham: Springer, 2014.

Otto, Rudolf. *The Idea of the Holy*. Translated by John W. Harvey. 2nd ed. Oxford: Oxford University Press, 1958.

Parrish, Stephen E. "Defending Theistic Conceptualism." *Philosophia Christi* 20 (2018) 101–17.

Parry, Robin A. [Gregory MacDonald, pseud.]. *The Evangelical Universalist*. 2nd ed. Eugene, OR: Cascade, 2012.

Perrine, Timothy. "Undermining Truthmaker Theory." *Synthese* 192 (2015) 185–200.

Perszyk, Ken. "Open Theism and the Soteriological Problem of Evil." In *Philosophical Essays against Open Theism*, edited by Benjamin H. Arbour, 159–77. New York: Routledge, 2019.

Peterson, Robert A. *Hell on Trial: The Case for Eternal Punishment*. Philipsburg, NJ: Presbyterian and Reformed, 1995.

Pinnock, Clark H. *Most Moved Mover: A Theology of God's Openness*. Grand Rapids: Baker Academic, 2001.

Plantinga, Alvin. "Can a Person Be a Soul?" *Closer to Truth*. https://www.closertotruth.com/series/can-person-be-soul#video-2840.

———. "On Ockham's Way Out." *Faith and Philosophy* 3 (1986) 235–69.

Bibliography

———. "Reply to Robert M. Adams." In *Alvin Plantinga*, edited by James E. Tomberlin and Peter van Inwagen, 371–85. Dordrecht: Reidel, 1985.

———. *Warranted Christian Belief*. Oxford: Oxford University Press, 2000.

Pojman, Louis P., and Lewis Vaughn. *Philosophy: The Quest for Truth*. 9th ed. Oxford: Oxford University Press, 2014.

Reitan, Eric. "A Guarantee of Universal Salvation?" *Faith and Philosophy* 24 (2007) 413–32.

Restall, Greg. "Molinism and the Thin Red Line." In *Molinism: The Contemporary Debate*, edited by Ken Perszyk, 227–38. Oxford: Oxford University Press, 2011.

Rice, Richard. *The Openness of God*. Minneapolis: Bethany House, 1985.

Rogers, Katherin A. "Eternity Has No Duration." *Religious Studies* 30 (1994) 1–16.

Salmela, Mikko. *True Emotions*. Consciousness & Emotions Book Series 9. Amsterdam: Benjamins, 2014.

Sanders, John. *The God Who Risks: A Theology of Providence*. Downers Grove, IL: InterVarsity, 1998.

Scrutton, Anastasia. "Living Like Common People: Emotion, Will, and Divine Passibility." *Religious Studies* 45 (2009) 373–93.

Shafer-Landau, Russ. *The Fundamentals of Ethics*. 2nd ed. Oxford: Oxford University Press, 2012.

Shedd, William G. T. *The Doctrine of Endless Punishment: Its Historical, Biblical and Rational Defense*. Reprint, Port St. Lucie, FL: Solid Ground Christian, 2010.

Shelton, W. Brian. *Prevenient Grace: God's Provision for Fallen Humanity*. Anderson, IN: Warner, 2014.

Stoffer, Dale R. *Background and Development of Brethren Doctrines, 1650–1987*. Philadelphia: Brethren Encyclopedia, 1989.

Strange, Daniel. "Universalism: Will Everyone Finally Be Saved?" *The Gospel Coalition*. https://www.thegospelcoalition.org/essay/universalism-will-everyone-finally-be-saved/.

Stratton, Timothy A. *Human Freedom, Divine Knowledge, and Mere Molinism: A Biblical, Historical, Theological, and Philosophical Analysis*. Eugene, OR: Wipf & Stock, 2020.

Stratton, Timothy A., and Jacobus Erasmus. "Mere Molinism: A Defense of Two Essential Pillars." *Perichoresis* 16 (2018) 17–29.

Swenson, Philip. "Ability, Foreknowledge, and Explanatory Dependence." *Australasian Journal of Philosophy* 94 (2016) 658–71.

———. "A Dilemma for Molinism." *YouTube*, August 19, 2021. http://youtube.com/watch?v=HEofxXY3hjE.

Swinburne, Richard. *Epistemic Justification*. Oxford: Clarendon, 2001.

Suárez, R. P. Francisci. *Opera Omnia*. Translated by Jacques-Paul Migne. 26 vols. Paris: Vivès, 1856–78.

Talbott, Thomas. *The Inescapable Love of God*. 2nd ed. Eugene, OR: Cascade, 2014.

Thomason, Richmond H., and Anil Gupta. "A Theory of Conditionals in the Context of Branching Time." In *Ifs*, edited by William L. Harper et al., 299–322. Dordrecht: Reidel, 1981.

Tillich, Paul. *Systematic Theology*. 3 vols. Chicago: University of Chicago Press, 1967.

Tolan, Stephanie S. "Intuition—The Mystery of Higher Intelligence." *Advanced Development* 18 (2020) 25–42.

Turri, John. "Is Knowledge Justified True Belief?" *Synthese* 184 (2012) 247–59.

Bibliography

Walton, John H. *The Lost World of Adam and Eve: Genesis 2–3 and the Human Origins Debate*. Downers Grove, IL: IVP Academic, 2015.

Welty, Greg. "Theistic Conceptual Realism." In *Beyond the Control of God? Six Views on the Problem of God and Abstract Objects*, edited by Paul Gould, 81–96. London: Bloomsbury, 2014.

Werther, David. "Open Theism and Middle Knowledge: An Appraisal of Gregory Boyd's Neo-Molinism." *Philosophia Christi* 5 (2003) 205–15.

Wevers, John William. "The First Book of the Kings." In *The Interpreter's One-Volume Commentary on the Bible*, edited by Charles M. Laymon, 181–96. Nashville: Abingdon, 1971.

Wierenga, Edward R. *The Nature of God: An Inquiry into Divine Attributes*. Cornell Studies in the Philosophy of Religion. Ithaca, NY: Cornell University Press, 2003.

Williams, J. Robert G. "Defending Conditional Excluded Middle." *Noûs* 44 (2010) 650–68.

Williamson, Timothy. "The Presidential Address: Armchair Philosophy, Metaphysical Modality, and Counterfactual Thinking." *Proceedings of the Aristotelian Society* 105 (2005) 1–23.

Wright, N. T. "The Letter to the Romans: Introduction, Commentary, and Reflections." In *The New Interpreter's Bible*, edited by Leander E. Keck, 10:393–770. Nashville: Abingdon, 2002.

Zagzebski, Linda Trinkaus. *The Dilemma of Freedom and Foreknowledge*. Oxford: Oxford University Press, 1991.

Subject Index

Abasciano, Brian J., 22, 139
abstract object, 55, 62, 70, 96, 146
A/C model, 108
A/C model, extended, 108
Ackermann, Fran, 48–49, 51, 142
actuality, xv, 91–92, 101, 106
actualization, strong, 16–21
actualization, weak, 16–21
Adams, Robert Merrihew, 40, 42, 46, 57–59, 65, 67–68, 74, 94, 139, 141, 145
ʾadôn, 9
ʾadōnāy, 9
aesthetics, theological, xv, 137
agency, 126
agglomeration step, 125
Alston, William P., 43–44, 48, 139
Anabaptism, 25, 117, 143
annihilationism, 15, 23, 121
anthropomorphism, xiv, 76–77
antinomianism, 118
apologetic, vii, xvi, 107, 112–13, 116, 135, 137, 142
Aquinas, Thomas. *See* Thomas Aquinas.
ara, 32
Arbour, Benjamin H., 144
archaeology, 7
Aristotle, 88, 125–27, 137, 141, 143
Armstrong, D. M., 54, 139

Arvan, Marcus, 136, 139
atheism, 66, 111
atonement, 28
Augustine, 25, 115, 139
Augustinian-Calvinist tradition, 25–26
axiological arguments, 6

backward causation, functional equivalent to, 55
Barth, Karl, xv, 107–9, 116, 140
Basil of Caesarea, 114, 140
Basinger, David, 45, 140
Bates, Matthew W., 28, 140
Bauer, Walter, 9–10, 140
beatific vision, 119–20, 126–28
Begbie, Jeremy S., 115, 140
beliefs, divine, xiv, 42–45, 48, 51–52, 54–56, 74, 79, 97, 135, 139
Belnap, Nuel, 100, 140, 144
Bengson, John, 48–49, 140
Boersma, Hans, 5, 140
Boethius, 132, 140
Booth, Anthony Robert, 48, 140, 143
Boyd, Gregory A., 45, 53–54, 76–77, 90, 132, 136–37, 140
branching time models, vii, xv, 91–92, 100, 102, 106, 135–37, 145
Braüner, Torben, 100, 140

Subject Index

Brethren, Church of the, 117–18, 142, 145
Brown, Francis, 8–9, 141
Bultmann, Rudolf, 7, 141

Calvin, John, 12, 14, 25, 108, 115, 141
Calvinist, 35–36
Campbell-Jack, W. C., 142
Carneades, 125–26, 137
causally unnecessary, 10
causation, agent, xiv, 71, 73, 125, 127–28, 133
certainty, 40, 51, 72, 75, 79
chance, 10–11, 43, 66, 117, 126
Chisholm, Roderick M., 71–72, 125–26, 141
Christ as art of God, 114
Christology, 8, 143
Church Fathers, 113
Clement of Alexandria, 113–14, 141
Climenhaga, Nevin, xiv, 59, 69–75, 136. 141
cognitive faculty, xiv, 42, 48, 51, 56, 108, 112, 135
Collins, John J., 26, 141
compatibilism, theological, 61, 109
compossible, 31, 86, 88, 105, 120
compound tenses, xv, 91, 99, 106
conceptualism, divine, 39, 41, 55, 96, 132, 144
conditional excluded middle (CEM), 46, 95, 136, 142, 146
consequentialism, 17, 120, 122–23
contingency, xiv, 10–11, 16, 19, 30, 41–42, 46–47, 68, 70, 72–75, 133–34, 137, 141–42
contradictories, 46, 95, 136
contraries, Stalnaker-Lewis, 46–47
control, divine, 9–11, 13, 16–17, 19, 87, 132, 146
Copan, Paul, 118, 144
cosmological arguments, 6, 142
counterfactuals, might, xv, 78, 132, 136–37
counterfactuals of creaturely freedom (CCFs), xiii–xiv, 34, 38–42, 49–51, 54–56, 61–64, 68, 71–77, 79, 86, 105, 131–33, 135–36

counterfactuals of divine emotion, 86, 88, 136
counterfactuals of divine freedom, 35, 52, 82, 88, 105
counterfactuals of indeterminacy, 93–95, 97, 99
counterfactuals, well-formed, 46, 95, 136
counterfactuals, would, 46, 86, 90, 132, 136
counterfactuals, would-probably, xv, 45, 77–80, 82–86, 89, 131
Craig, William Lane, 19, 22, 30, 33, 36, 38–39, 41, 46–48, 52, 58–59, 64, 69–70, 72–73, 78, 94–98, 108, 110, 112, 124, 126–28, 131–32, 137, 141–42, 144
creatio continuans, 131
creatio ex nihilo, 131
creation, xiv, 6–7, 15, 21, 24, 29, 31, 34, 71–72, 87, 109, 120, 129, 131, 134
Cross, Charles B., 46, 142

Daigle, Lauren, 111
damnation, transworld, 30, 105, 123–24
Davis, Charles C., 97, 144
death, spiritual, 14–15
decision, divine creative, 37, 57, 82, 85, 89
decision, fully informed, 126–28, 133
dehumanization, 123
deliberation, absolutely complete and unlimited, 53, 110
Demey, Lorenz, 137, 142
demythologization, 7
deontology, 122
dependence, conceptual, 60–61
dependence, counterfactual, 61
dependence, explanatory, 59–61, 145
dependence, genuine counterfactual, 61–62, 64
dependence, logical, 35, 60
dependence, ontological, 131
despotēs, 9
determinism, xiv, 41–42, 53, 55–56, 61, 75, 100, 109, 140
Dickinson, Travis M., 43–45, 142
disquotation principle, 39, 96
divine changes of mind, xiv, 76–77, 82–85

Subject Index

divine confrontation of the unexpected, xv, 77, 80–81, 89, 131
divine regret, xiv–xv, 76–77, 85–89
divine relational changeability texts, 14, 77, 135–36
divine repentance, xiv–xv, 76–77, 85–89
divine testing of human character, xv, 76–77, 81–82, 89
Doctrine of Double Effect (DDE), 16, 122
Dörfler, Viktor, 48–49, 51, 142
Doyle, Bob, 125–26, 142
dualism, substance, 48
dunasthai, 12
Durnbaugh, Donald F., 118, 142
dynastēs, 9

Eastern Orthodoxy, 25
Edgar, William, 113, 142
efficacious, 107, 109–10
Egler, Miguel, 48–50, 142
elect, 22–23, 29–33, 37, 139
emotions, genuinely irreconcilable, 88
emotions, *prima facie* irreconcilable, 88
enabling condition, 66–67
enlightenment, 7, 26–28
Epicurus, 125–27
epistemic notion, 72
epistemological evidence, 93
epistemologists, 51, 112
Epstein, Richard L., 94, 142
equivocation, 59, 61, 66, 74–75, 101
Erasmus, Jacobus, 134, 145
Erickson, Millard J., 45, 142
essence, creaturely libertarian (CLE), 45–47, 50, 52–53, 56
essence, individual, 23, 39, 41–42, 45
eternalism, xvi, 64, 119–30, 134
eternality, divine, 52
evangelism, 118
existence of God, 6, 113
existentialism, 7
expectation, 82–83, 85, 89
explanation, full, 69–73, 75
explanatory loop, 65–66, 68, 75
explanatory priority, vii, xiv, 57–75, 142
explanatory priority, transitive, 57–59, 61, 65, 67–69, 74, 142

explanatory priority, univocal, 59–60, 142

facts, contingent, xiv, 70, 72–75
facts, hard, 62–63
facts, soft, 62
faith, 5, 15, 22–23, 28, 140–41, 144
false-maker, 96–97
feasibility, xv, 91, 99, 106
Fitzwater, Aaron, 30, 105
Fixity of the Independent, xiv, 59–64, 69, 74, 143
Flint, Thomas P., 46–47, 58–59, 63, 65–66, 68, 88, 98, 142
foreknowledge, 19, 22–23, 29–31, 34–35, 39–42, 46–47, 52–54, 64, 66, 73, 79, 96, 110, 131–33, 135, 140–42, 144–46
foreknowledge of hypothetical conditionals, 17, 29–32, 34, 37, 39, 110
Frankfurt-style counterexamples, 11
Freddoso, Alfred J., 46–47, 142, 144
freedom, divine, 35, 40, 52–54, 66, 82, 88, 105, 132
freedom, human, xiii, 1, 8, 11–17, 21, 24–25, 34, 36, 40, 53, 59, 62, 64, 66, 70–75, 123–35, 141, 143, 145
freedom, libertarian, xiv, xvi, 1, 11–12, 25–26, 35–36, 38, 45, 62, 107–10, 119, 122, 124–37
fruit of the Spirit, 6–7
future, feasible, xv, 98–99, 101, 103, 105, 136
future, possible, xv, 136
futurefactual, 52, 64

Gæbelein, Frank E., 142
galaxy, possible, 98–99, 101–5, 131–33
Gaskin, Richard, 46, 142
Gettier counterexamples, 51–52
gifts, spiritual, 3
ginōskō, 22
Gould, Paul, 146
grace, xiii, 1, 8, 12, 21, 24, 25–29, 32, 34, 36–37, 118, 120, 126, 128, 135
grace, prevenient, 26–28, 31–32, 36, 145
Great Commission, 14, 28, 118

Subject Index

grounded, ontologically, 1–2, 4
grounding objection, xiii, 36, 38–42, 56, 74, 91–101, 135–36, 141, 143
Grudem, Wayne, 13, 87, 142
Gupta, Anil, 100, 145

habitudes, 41–42
Harper, William L., 145
Harrison, Everett F., 26, 142
Harvey, John W., 144
Hasker, William, 41, 54, 57–59, 63, 65, 69, 74, 141–42
Hays, Richard B., 22, 121, 142
Heidegger, Martin, 7
hell, xvi, 15, 23, 26, 117–22, 127–28, 130, 134, 137, 144
Hess, Elijah, 46, 132–33, 136–37, 142
heuristic device, xv, 37, 77, 92, 136
holiness, 107
holos, 28

idea, 23, 41–42, 55, 74
imagination, divine, 39, 51
imago Dei, 48, 107, 135
impassibility, divine, 87, 143
impossibility, psychological, 129–30
infallibility, divine, 44
influence, 69–74, 87, 127
interpretation, biblical, vii, xvi, 1, 7, 22, 26, 30, 35, 76–90, 119, 133
intuition, divine, vii, xiv, 38, 42, 47–52, 56, 135
intuition, human, xiv, 48–51, 123, 135, 140, 142–45
intuition, phenomenology of, 48–49

Jehovah's Witnesses, 2
Johnson, Michael, 48, 143
justification, xiv, 51–52, 56, 78, 111, 126, 129, 145

Kahneman, Daniel, 48, 50, 143
kataluma, 7
Keck, Leander E., 146
knowledge, counterfactual, 51
knowledge, free, 35–37, 52–53, 57, 82, 84–86, 88

knowledge, logical structure of natural, 77–80
knowledge, middle, xv, 19, 33–42, 46, 51–53, 57, 60, 63, 68, 72, 75, 77–86, 88, 90, 97–98, 103, 110, 116, 122, 124, 130–32, 134, 137, 139–43, 146
knowledge, natural, xv, 34–35, 37, 53, 57, 60, 77–86, 89, 97, 102, 131–32
knowledge, prevolitional, 38, 53–54, 68, 78, 110, 132
knowledge, prior relational, 23
Koksvik, Ole, 48–49, 143
kosmos, 13, 27–28
Kowalski, Dean A., 46, 143
Kristjánsson, Kristján, 88, 143
Kvanvig, Jonathan L., 41, 93, 125, 143

Laing, John D., 40–42, 46, 52–54, 56, 74, 143
Law, Andrew, 59–63, 143
laws of logic, 34, 131
Laymon, Charles M., 146
Leftow, Brian, 132, 143
letummō, 10
Lewis, David, xv, 46–47, 87, 93, 136, 139, 143
Lewis, Gordon, 87, 143
likelihood, 72
literal, xiv–xv, 3, 22, 30, 76–77, 80–82, 85–86, 88–90, 92, 105, 136
Logos, 3, 7–8
Louw, Johannes P., 9, 143
Lowe, E. J., 50, 143
Luther, Martin, 12, 25, 143

MacDonald, Gregory. *See* Parry, Robin A.
MacGregor, Kirk R., 14–20, 22–23, 25–26, 30–33, 37, 39–40, 51, 54–55, 76–78, 96, 108, 114, 142–43
Mack, Alexander, 118, 143
Malpass, Alex, xv, 91–101, 105–6, 143
Manis, R. Zachary, xvi, 119–24, 129–30, 144
Matava, R. J., 41–42, 46, 144
McClymond, Michael, 118, 144
McKim, Vaughn R., 97, 144

Subject Index

metalepsis, 22, 121
metaphorical, xv, 27, 76–77, 80–86, 89, 136
Milne, Peter, 39, 144
mind, divine, xiv, 4, 41, 74
modal logic, 46
modal notion, 70, 72, 75
Molina, Luis de, xv–xvi, 16–17, 19–20, 22–23, 30–33, 37–41, 47, 51–54, 56, 78–79, 88–89, 96, 99–100, 107–8, 110, 116, 118, 135–37, 142–44
Molinist, xii–xvi, 1, 21, 23, 33–37, 42, 55, 58, 62–63, 68–69, 71, 74–77, 80–91, 96, 100–101, 117, 119–20, 124, 134, 137, 139, 141–43
moral law, universal, 6
Moreland, J. P., 15, 48, 70, 78, 122–23, 126–27, 131, 144
Müller, Thomas, 140, 144
music, vii, xv–xvi, 107, 109–16, 135, 137, 140, 142
music, holy, xv–xvi, 107, 109–16, 137
music, non-holy, xv, 107, 113
music, sacred, 107, 109
music, secular, 107, 109
Muslims, 2

Nado, Jennifer, 48, 143
necessary condition, 5, 34, 60
necessitas consequentiae, 46, 70, 75
necessitas consequentis, 46, 70, 75
necessity, 10, 41–42, 46, 54, 60, 66, 72, 75, 126
Nida, Eugene A., 9, 143
noetic priority, 65, 67–68
non-feasible universalist world hypothesis (NFUW), 119–24
numbers, 131, 140

objective moral values, 131
OCD, 16
Øhrstrøm, Peter, 99–100, 144
omnibenevolence, 8, 17, 119, 133
omnipotence, 32, 36, 40, 111, 128
omniscience, 17, 32, 34–37, 42, 52, 97, 102, 141

ontological conclusion, 93
open theism, vii, xiv, 45, 47, 53–54, 66, 76–90, 125, 130–34, 136–37, 140–41, 144, 146
Otto, Rudolf, 107, 144

paradigm, Augustinian-Calvinistic, 22–23
paradigm, intertextual Jewish, 22
Parrish, Stephen E., 41, 144
Parry, Robin A., 23, 26, 126, 130, 134, 144
partial reason for, 66–67
past, actual, xv, 91, 98
past, nonactual, xv, 91
Perrine, Timothy, 39, 144
Perszyk, Ken, 125, 130, 133–34, 144–45
Peterson, Robert A., 134, 144
phenomenology, 48–49
phenomenology, presentational, 49
philosophical constructs, genuine, 1, 6–8
philosophical constructs, human-made, 1, 6–7
philosophy and theology, proper relationship between, xiii, 1–8
Pinnock, Clark H., 45, 140, 144
Plantinga, Alvin, xv, 51, 62, 67–68, 93–94, 107–8, 112, 116–17, 144–45
Platonism, 114
Pojman, Louis P., 112, 141, 145
possibility, xv, 10, 29–30, 55, 73, 77–78, 91, 99, 106, 119, 124, 126, 129–30, 137, 143
power, causal, 54, 73, 94
power over the past, counterfactual, 55
predestination, xiii, xvi, 1, 8, 21–25, 27–34, 135
presence, definitive, 120–21
presence, divine, xvi, 111, 116, 121
presence, repletive, 15, 121–22
presuppositions, metaphysical, 5
probability, intrinsic, xv, 47, 49, 77–81, 83–86, 89, 125, 129, 131–32, 136
probability, nonzero, 124–25, 129
proginōskō, 22
prognōsis, 22
properly basic beliefs, 108
properties, accidental, 41–42
properties, contingent, 41

Subject Index

properties, necessary, 41
proposition, type N, 45–47, 49, 51, 54, 56
proposition, type P, 45–47, 49, 51, 54, 56
Protestantism, 25
providence, xvi, 18, 59, 63, 65–66, 88, 98, 124, 135, 141–42, 145
psychic ability, 50

random, 10–11, 78, 94, 124–31, 133
Reformation, 115
Reitan, Eric, xvi, 119, 124–27, 129–30, 145
reprobate, 23, 29–33, 37, 117
Restall, Greg, 100, 145
resurrection of Jesus, 19, 31, 113
Rice, Richard, 54, 145
risk-taking, 133
Rogers, Katherin A., 94, 97, 145
Roman Catholicism, 25
Rooney, Michael, 94, 142
Rowbottom, Daniel P., 48, 140, 143
Rubio, Daniel, xiv, 59, 69–75, 136, 141

Salmela, Mikko, 88, 145
salvation, optimal, 32–33, 37, 89, 119–20, 122
salvation, universal, 33, 119, 125, 127, 129–31, 145
salvific will, divine, 21, 28–33, 135
Sanders, John, 45, 145
Scrutton, Anastasia, 87, 145
second coming, 28, 63
segment, feasible, 99
segment, possible, 99
self-autonomy, 128
self-bondage, 128
self-deception, 128
sensus divinitatis, xvi, 108–12, 115–16, 137
Sermon on the Mount, 14
Shafer-Landau, Russ, 16, 145
shalliyt, 8
Shedd, William G. T., 134, 145
Shelton, W. Brian, 26–28, 145
shōltan, 8
sin, original, 25–26
social justice, 118
sola fide, 118
songs, new, 114

songs, old, 114
soul-creationism, 120
soul, divine, 48
soul, faculties of, 15
soul, human, 9, 14–16, 23, 25, 48, 113–14, 117, 119–20, 144
sovereignty, divine, xiii, 1, 8–11, 16–19, 21, 31, 135, 143
Stalnaker-Lewis semantics, xv, 46–47, 93, 136
Stoffer, Dale R., 118, 145
Strange, Daniel, 118, 145
Stratton, Timothy A., 12, 134, 145
Strobel, Lee, 123, 144
Suárez, R. P. Francisci, xiii, 41–42, 46–47, 52, 56, 141, 143, 145
sufficient condition, 36, 45, 60, 65–67, 69, 75, 94, 134
supercomprehension, vii, xiv, 38–56, 74, 143
Swenson, Philip, xiv, 59–70, 74–75, 136, 145
Swinburne, Richard, 77–78, 129, 145
symmetric relation, 60, 69
symmetry, acausal, 55, 73–74, 136

Talbott, Thomas, 23, 26, 126–29, 133–34, 141, 145
Tarski, Alfred, 38
tautologies, 97–98
theodicy, 124
theology, perfect being, 41–47, 51, 56, 65
theology, philosophical, xvi, 38, 41, 119, 121, 143
thin red line, 93, 97–100, 103–5, 131, 133, 143–45
Thomas Aquinas, 2, 108, 114, 139, 143
Thomason, Richmond H., 100, 145
Tillich, Paul, 121, 145
time, absolute, 94–95
time, A-Theory of, 64, 92, 131–32
time, B-Theory of, 64, 92, 131–32
time, passage of, 94
time, relational, 94–95
timelessness, divine, 42, 52–53, 64, 89, 94, 132, 136
Tolan, Stephanie S., 48, 50–51, 145

Subject Index

traditionalism, 23
traducianism, 120
trinitarian being of God, 14, 115
Trinity, 8, 114, 129
truth, contingent, 72
truth, necessary, xv, 34, 37, 63, 72, 78
truthmakers, 38–39, 42, 51, 54–56, 74, 96–97, 99, 135, 139, 144
Turri, John, 51, 145

Ultimate Being, 2
uncertainty, intrinsic, 79
unchangeability of divine intentions, xiv, 68–69
underdeterminative, evidentially, xiv, 42, 47–49, 52, 56, 135
universalism, eventual, 117–19, 124–26, 128–35, 137
universe, block, 131–32

Vaughn, Lewis, 112, 141, 145

Walton, John H., 15, 146
warrant, xiv, 51–52, 56, 108, 112, 145
Wawer, Jacek, 100, 143
Welty, Greg, 55, 146

Werther, David, 78, 146
Wevers, John William, 10, 146
Wierenga, Edward R., 93, 146
will, preexistent, 74–75
Williams, J. Robert G., 136, 146
Williamson, Timothy, 49–50, 146
wisdom, earthly, 18, 21
wisdom from above, 2
wisdom, human, 2, 6
wisdom of the world, 2, 5
Word of God, 108–9
world, feasible, xv, 31–35, 37, 62–63, 88, 92, 99, 103–5, 119–20, 122–24, 128–33, 136
world, possible, 34, 37, 61, 73, 91, 93–95, 98–99, 102–3
world, salvifically optimal feasible, 37, 120, 122
worship, faithful, 115
would, modal conception of, 100
Wright, N. T., 26, 146

yāda', 22

Zagzebski, Linda Trinkaus, 42, 146

Scripture Index

OLD TESTAMENT

Genesis
2:7	15
2:9	15
3	11, 36
3:22–24	15
6:5–6	86, 88, 131
6:6	76
22	81–82
22:12	76, 82
37:23–24	18
37:25–28	18
37:31–33	18
39:14–18	18
39:20	18
40:9–15	18
40:20–21	18
40:23	18
50:20	19

Exodus
32:9–14	76, 82–84

Deuteronomy
8:2–21	76
11:26–28	12
13:1–3	76
30:11–19	11–12

Judges
3:4	76

1 Samuel
13:13	76
15:10	76
15:11	86, 89
15:35	76
23:9–13	17

1 Kings
3:28	3
4:29	3
5:12	3
10:24	3
22:34	10

1 Chronicles
21:15	76

Scripture Index

2 Chronicles

9:3	3
9:23	3
18:33	10
32:31	76

Ezra

1:1	10
6:22	10
7:25	3

Job

1:9–12	81
1:20–22	81
3:16	122
12:13	3
38:36	3

Psalms

8:9	9
103:14	15
104:24	3
145:9	29

Proverbs

2:1–6	4
3:19	3
4:5–8	4
7:4	4
8:17	4
8:22–31	3
9:4–6	4
14:5	10
16:1	17
16:9	17
16:16	4
16:22	4
16:33	10
20:24	10
21:1	10
23:33	4
26:10	10

Isaiah

1:24	9
3:1	9
5:2–5	45, 76
10:16	9
10:33	9
11:2	3
19:4	9
28:29	3
29:16	24
38:1–5	76, 84–85
45:9	24
47:10	7
49:6	29
51:22	9
55:1–3	13
55:6–7	13
63:8–10	45, 76

Jeremiah

3:3–20	45, 76
3:19–20	80
7:31	76
10:12	3
10:23	10
18:4–11	76
20:14–18	121–22
26:7–19	76
32:35	45, 76, 80
38:17–18	17
51:15	3

Lamentations

3:33	17

Ezekiel

18:23	13, 28
18:30–32	13, 28
22:30–31	45, 76
28:17	6
33:11	13, 28
36:26–27	13

Scripture Index

Daniel

2:20–21	2
4:3	8
4:17	8
4:25	8
4:32	8
4:34	8
5:21	8

Joel

2:12–13	76

Jonah

3:9—4:2	76

NEW TESTAMENT

Matthew

7:24–27	14
11:19	3
11:20–24	17, 30, 35, 105
11:27	21–22
22:14–16	19
23:34	3
26:24	121
26:47–49	19
28:19–20	14
28:19	28–29

Mark

6:2	3
14:10–11	19
14:43–46	19

Luke

2:7	7
2:40	3
7:35	3
10:13–15	17, 30
10:22	22
10:31	10
11:49	3
22:3–6	19
22:47–48	19

John

1:1–14	7
1:1–2	3
1:9	26–27
1:10	7
1:14	7
3:16–17	13
6	24–25
6:44	25
6:45	25
6:65	25
11:47–53	19
14:8–10	25
15:22–24	17
18:33–38	19
18:36	17

Acts

2:23–24	19
4:24	9
4:27–28	19
13:48	21
17:26–27	10

Romans

1:20	6
2:4	27
2:6–11	27–28
2:14–16	6
4	28
5:12–21	26
5:15	26
5:18–19	26
8:28	17–18
8:29–30	22–23
9	22–23, 139
9:11–18	23
9:11–13	32
9:16	31
9:19–24	24
9:19	24
9:20	24
11:11–12	29
11:25–26	29
11:30–32	29
12:21	18

Scripture Index

1 Corinthians

1:20–25	5–6
1:20	2
1:24	3
1:30	3
2:1	6
2:4	6
2:5	6
2:6–7	4–5
2:6	5
2:8	17
2:13	2
3:15	32
3:19	6
8:1–3	6
10:13	12
12:8	3

2 Corinthians

1:12	2
5:18–21	19
10:4–5	6–7

Galatians

3:6–9	28

Ephesians

1:4–5	21
1:8–9	3
1:11	17–18
1:17–19	7
1:17	3
2:1–2	14
2:1	14–15
2:3–5	24
2:3	14
2:5	14
2:12	15
3:10	5
3:17	15
3:18	15

Colossians

1:16	3
1:28	4
2:4	3
2:8	5
3:16	4

1 Thessalonians

1:4	21

2 Thessalonians

2:13	21

1 Timothy

2:3–4	28
6:15	9

Titus

2:11	26

James

1:5	3
1:17	6
3:14–16	5
3:17	2

1 Peter

1:1–2	22–23

2 Peter

3:9	28

Revelation

6:10	9

www.ingramcontent.com/pod-product-compliance
Lightning Source LLC
Chambersburg PA
CBHW052100230426
43662CB00036B/1711